THE LIFE-CHANGING POWER OF
Prayer

T. W. HUNT

LifeWay Press
Nashville, Tennessee

ISBN 0-6330-1980-1

This book is the text for course CG-0789 in the subject area Prayer
in the Christian Growth Study Plan.

Dewey Decimal Classification Number: 248.32
Subject Heading: PRAYER

Unless otherwise indicated, all Scripture quotations are from
the NEW AMERICAN STANDARD BIBLE, © Copyright The Lockman Foundation,
1960, 1962, 1963, 1968, 1971, 1972, 1973, 1975, 1977. Used by permission.

Scripture quotations identified KJV are from the *King James Version*.

Scripture quotations identified NIV are from the Holy Bible, *New International Version,*
copyright © 1973, 1978, 1984 by International Bible Society.

We believe the Bible has God for its author; salvation for its end; and truth,
without any mixture of error, for its matter and that all Scripture is totally true
and trustworthy. The 2000 statement of *The Baptist Faith and Message* is our doctrinal guideline.

To order additional copies of this resource, write to LifeWay Church Resources Customer Service;
One LifeWay Plaza; Nashville, TN 37234-0013; fax (615) 251-5933; phone toll free (800) 458-2772;
email *customerservice@lifeway.com;* order online at *www.lifeway.com;* or visit the LifeWay Christian Store serving you.

Printed in the United States of America

Leadership and Adult Publishing
LifeWay Church Resources
One LifeWay Plaza
Nashville, TN 37234-0175

Contents

About the Author

T. W. Hunt is known around the world as a teacher, a writer, and a man of prayer. He has given his life to teaching others the ways of God. For 24 years he taught music and missions at Southwestern Baptist Theological Seminary in Fort Worth, Texas. He served for 7 years as the prayer consultant for LifeWay Christian Resources of the Southern Baptist Convention.

Born in Mammoth Spring, Arkansas, T. W. is a graduate of Ouachita Baptist University and holds master of music and doctor of philosophy degrees from North Texas State University. He has made a lifelong study of prayer and the ways God makes Himself known to us. His understanding and insight have been forged from the furnace of real life. T. W. practices what he preaches.

T. W. has written numerous books and courses of study, including *Music in Missions: Discipling Through Music, Disciple's Prayer Life: Walking in Fellowship with God* (with Catherine Walker), *In God's Presence: Your Daily Guide to a Meaningful Prayer Life* (with Claude King), *The Mind of Christ* (with Claude King), and *From Heaven's View: God Bringing His Children to Glory* (with his daughter, Melana).

T. W. has circled the world countless times teaching missions leaders, missionaries, and national church leaders in many countries. He conducts seminars for denominational leaders, pastors, other church leaders, and laypersons in churches and denominational assemblies throughout the United States.

T. W. has been married to his childhood sweetheart, Laverne, for more than 50 years. They have one daughter, Melana; a son-in-law, Steve Monroe; and six grandchildren. T. W. and Laverne make their home in Spring, Texas.

T. W. regularly prays for those who may be studying this book. As you study, T. W. is asking the Father to give you understanding and guidance so that you might know God's will for your life more fully and be richly blessed as you walk in that will.

Preface to the
Second Edition

The startling increase in the practice of prayer since I began teaching on prayer many years ago has been awe-inspiring to those of us who anxiously desire that God be the motivating agent for all the work of His church. Most denominations now have prayer leaders, and in some denominations their principal departments or agencies have offices devoted to the promotion of prayer. In many cases state or regional denominational headquarters have prayer arms. *Pray* magazine is informing laypersons and the clergy about prayer on a greater scale than Christianity has known. Christian magazines are offering more articles on prayer and related articles, such as healing. Even national newsmagazines have devoted their lead stories to prayer. The gradual but steady increase in this work of prayer indicates that God Himself has stepped into the ordering of His church's direction.

For this reason it was gratifying to learn that LifeWay Press wanted to issue a revision of my 1986 book *The Doctrine of Prayer*—and even offered an incredible amount of help to facilitate the process. Dr. Art Criscoe's learning activities in this volume are outstanding. He also found helpful illustrations in some of my other studies to clarify certain points. My editor, David Haney, has saved me hours as he skillfully reedited the material and suggested ways to improve this new edition. I worked with both of these men during my years at LifeWay and came to trust their spirituality and editing skills.

You will quickly notice that the teachings in this book directly derive from the prayers of the Bible. Twice I have typed all of the prayers of the Bible into my computer in different translations and have tried to base my thinking and practice of prayer on those hard-copy printings. Basing my own prayers on biblical prayers has profoundly deepened my reverence for God and has led me to pray with more dependence on the Holy Spirit. One result has been more frequent affirmative answers to my requests of God. Most important, the prayers of the Bible have intensified my desire to identify with Christ and to seek God's purposes above all else. I pray that the same thing happens to you as you read and apply the teachings in this book.

Preface to the
First Edition

So many writers, preachers, and teachers have influenced my prayer life and my understanding of prayer that it would be impossible to list them or credit them properly. Prayer is an ancient subject and has gripped the attention of minds and spirits far greater than mine throughout history. But there is one credit I cannot ignore. Years ago I met a man of prayer of such great faith that I constantly remained astonished as I got to know him. His name was Bob Maulden.

Bob kept a prayer room in his home and in his business, a Christian bookstore. I quickly learned that he was available to pray at any hour of the day or night. Sometimes I would call him with a prayer request, and he would turn over a sale to a clerk in order to begin praying immediately. He was at his church every Sunday morning at 6:00 a.m. and would pray until other people began to arrive. His widow, Bea, also a prayer warrior to whom I am greatly indebted, told me that many times Bob prayed all night. I had never known anyone so completely given to prayer. Bob's faith so intrigued me that I began studying the prayers of the Bible, and my own prayer life was transformed. Bob went to be with the Lord in February of 1982, but his legacy lives on in the lives of many who were changed by the power of his prayers. I am one of those, and this book is gratefully dedicated to him.

Another prayerful couple in Fort Worth made this book possible by the gift of the computer and word processor on which this book was written. It would have been impossible without their gift and their prayers, but they prefer to remain anonymous. Still, I must acknowledge a profound debt to their enabling.

My wife and my daughter patiently read the manuscript; made helpful suggestions; and most importantly, upheld me with the best support anyone can give—prayer. And every day of my life I have been prayed for by the two persons who were God's instrument to give me physical life and to lead me into eternal life—my parents. This book owes much to my family.

My supreme debt is to the Father of Light who gives light. Even the people who have blessed me were His gift to me. He is the source of my knowledge and of the insights of my teachers. My prayer is that when God's people read this book, they will see the validity of His method and will grant Him the pleasure He has asked throughout time—the pleasure of their company.

Chapter 1
The Foundation of Prayer: The God Who Cares

From the soft voice of a child's first prayer to the whispered prayer of an aged Christian's last breath, prayer is the greatest privilege of life and is the greatest source of power on earth.

Prayer is many things. Talking with God. Listening to God. Communicating. Asking and receiving. Above all, prayer is a relationship. It is not one-sided communication with a distant God. Prayer is a conversation between us and God, a relationship between us and our Creator. God desires our fellowship. More than anything else, He wants us to love Him with all our being: " 'Love the Lord your God with all your heart and with all your soul and with all your might' " (Deut. 6:5). He also wants us to know and experience His love and presence. God is seeking that kind of relationship with each of us.

Prayer is a relationship.

Prayer is the cry of the human heart to the great God of the universe. Prayer is the voice of a child to the loving Heavenly Father. Prayer is the expression of our need to the loving Father, who is ready to help. Prayer is inviting God, who always has time, into the midst of our busy lives. Prayer is a precious gift from God that gives us the right and privilege of talking with Him anytime, anywhere. We can express our love and adoration for Him and share every need and concern we have at any time. The door is always open. God will always listen. And He will answer.

◖(◕◍◕)◗

Before you begin your study, turn back to the contents page and read again the chapter headings. Briefly state what you hope to gain from this study.

_____

_____

Write a question you have about prayer that you would like to be answered during your study.

_____

Now spend a few minutes in prayer asking God to make Himself known to you in a very intimate way as you study this book. Ask that your study will become a life-changing experience as you discover the significance and power of prayer.

Prayer Is Universal

Prayer is as old as humankind, permeates all of history, and is common to all people. Humans are unique among God's creatures. Made in the likeness of God, they alone are in a condition to have fellowship with God. We read in the Bible about men praying (Hezekiah, Paul), women praying (Miriam, Anna), and children praying (Samuel, Josiah). Scripturally, prayer is universal in time and in space.

Universal in time. Genesis pictures God introducing Adam to His world. Evidently, the Lord and Adam walked together, talked together, and enjoyed a sharing that is characteristic of beings with common interests. There can be no doubt that Adam enjoyed an unspoiled fellowship with God prior to his fall. That sort of dialogue can perhaps be called a type of prayer. Surely Abel also, who knew how to offer a sacrifice pleasing to God, must have addressed some sort of prayer to God. After Abel's murder God gave Eve a son, Seth, whose name means *appointed;* that is, he was appointed in the place of Abel (see Gen. 4:25). It was through this line (not Cain's line but through the replacement for righteous Abel) that a significant new dimension of fellowship with God was introduced into human history.

To Seth was born Enosh, whose name means *man* or even *weakness* or *mortality.* Adam means *man*, generically as human, but now man is Enosh, man in his weakness. As the slowly developing awareness of the dreadful separation sin had imposed permeated the consciousness of this new generation, a sense of yearning and need moved people to reach out to the only source that could meet that need. To Enosh, to one who was frail and realized his

"Prayer, to the patriarchs and prophets, was more than the recital of well-known and well-worn phrases— it was the outpouring of the heart."[1]
—Herbert Lockyer (1902–73), Scottish pastor and Bible teacher

dependence on God, was granted the privilege of marking an important milestone in prayer history: "To Seth, to him also a son was born; and he called his name Enosh. Then men began to call upon the name of the Lord" (Gen. 4:26). The Hebrew word *call* (*qara*) is a strong verb of action. It means *to cry out, to call aloud*. Rather than just a random outcry, *qara* is usually used to address a specific person in order to make a specific request. People used this word throughout the Old Testament to cry out to God for His help.[2]

This calling on the name of the Lord would characterize God's people from the time of Enosh onward. As Abram trekked across the Fertile Crescent and down into the land of Canaan, years before his name was changed to Abraham, he called on the name of the Lord (see Gen. 12:8). So consistent and faithful was Abraham in his prayer life and his walk with God that he was called God's friend (see 1 Chron. 20:7; Isa. 41:8; Jas. 2:23).

So consistent and faithful was Abraham in his prayer life and his walk with God that he was called God's friend.

In Moses' moving farewell message on the plains of Moab to the people he had nurtured and led for so many years, he urged them to stay close to God and obey His commandments. He reminded them of the difference between the Lord God and the gods of the surrounding peoples: " 'What great nation is there that has a god so near to it as is the Lord our God whenever we call on Him?' " (Deut. 4:7). Many generations later in another emotional address reminiscent of the one Moses gave, the aged Samuel admonished the people to obey God and follow Him (see 1 Sam. 12). Jabez "called on the God of Israel" (1 Chron. 4:10) and made his brief petition, which God granted. In Elijah's great contest with Baal he called on the Lord (see 1 Kings 18:24).

David called on the Lord and later praised Him for delivering him from Saul and his other enemies:

"I call upon the Lord, who is worthy to be praised;
And I am saved from my enemies" (2 Sam. 22:4).

David was bold in his praying; he was not at all hesitant in approaching God:

Answer me when I call, O God of my righteousness!
Thou hast relieved me in my distress;
Be gracious to me and hear my prayer (Ps. 4:1).

David purchased a Jebusite threshing floor, the site where the temple would be built years later, and built an altar on it. After he offered sacrifices, "He called to the Lord and He answered him with fire from heaven on the altar of burnt offering" (1 Chron. 21:26).

In Psalm 55 the king had been betrayed by a trusted and intimate friend. In his hurt and pain from his colleague's treachery, David called on God in prayer:

As for me, I shall call upon God,
And the Lord will save me.
Evening and morning and at noon, I will complain and murmur,
And He will hear my voice (Ps. 55:16-17).

Knowing firsthand God's forgiveness for sin, David could pray:

Thou, Lord, art good, and ready to forgive,
And abundant in lovingkindness to all who call upon Thee (Ps. 86:5).

Psalm 102 is the earnest plea of a person undergoing great affliction and trouble:

Hear my prayer, O Lord!
And let my cry for help come to Thee.
Do not hide Thy face from me in the day of my distress;
Incline Thine ear to me;
In the day when I call answer me quickly (Ps. 102:1-2).

Psalm 105 recounts the history of God's care for Israel. It begins with a proclamation for people to call on God:

Give thanks to the Lord, call upon His name;
Make known His deeds among the peoples.
Sing to Him, sing praises to Him;
Speak of all His wonders (Ps. 105:1-2).

Psalm 145 gives a precious promise to all who call on God:

The Lord is near to all who call upon Him,
To all who call upon Him in truth (Ps. 145:18).

Psalm 116 is a song of personal thanksgiving for answered prayer:

I love the Lord, because He hears
My voice and my supplications.
Because He has inclined His ear to me,
Therefore I shall call upon Him as long as I live (Ps. 116:1-2).

God Himself invites us to call on Him and assures us of His help:

Call upon Me in the day of trouble;
I shall rescue you, and you will honor Me (Ps. 50:15).

Isaiah also urged his listeners to

Seek the Lord while He may be found;
Call upon Him while He is near (Isa. 55:6).

Indignation threatens those who do not call on the Lord:

Pour out Thy wrath upon the nations which do not know Thee,
And upon the kingdoms which do not call upon Thy name (Ps. 79:6).

Have the workers of wickedness no knowledge,
Who eat up My people as though they ate bread,
And have not called upon God (Ps. 53:4)?

> *"He will call upon Me,*
> *and I will answer him;*
> *I will be with him*
> *in trouble;*
> *I will rescue him, and*
> *honor him" (Ps. 91:15).*

The practice of calling on God in prayer continued throughout the entire biblical period. In the New Testament that calling out to God became a calling out to Christ. The Greek root word *kaleo*, meaning *to call,* is a common New Testament word. Our word *church* (*ekklesia*), which means *the called-out ones,* comes from that root word. Peter's sermon at Pentecost, quoting Joel's prophecy of universal opportunity for salvation (see Joel 2:32), promises that whoever calls on the name of the Lord will be saved (see Acts 2:21). Paul addressed his first Corinthian letter to "all who in every place call upon the name of our Lord Jesus Christ" (1 Cor. 1:2).

From the dawn of history, then, the greatest men and women—Moses, Abraham, Hannah, Mary—were people of prayer. From Genesis to Malachi, from Matthew to Revelation, the biblical record shows that the saints consistently prayed. The next-to-last

Throughout the Bible, prayer sustained the people of God.

verse in the Bible is a prayer (see Rev. 22:20). Throughout the Bible, prayer sustained the people of God.

Calling out to God in prayer did not end with biblical history. It has continued through the centuries, wherever Christians have been found. Autobiographies and biographies of great Christians are filled with thrilling accounts of ways people have called out to God and received His help. John Paton from Scotland was a missionary to the islands of the South Pacific in the late 1800s. Working for years on an island where the natives were very fierce cannibals, he was always safe because he remained in prayer to God. One night Paton's dog awoke him. Sensing danger, Paton got up and awoke a missionary couple staying with him. They immediately began praying. Suddenly they saw men with torches outside the window. The church beside the house was in flames, and the fire was traveling toward the house along a reed fence. Paton ran outside and found himself surrounded by warriors with raised clubs. He wrote:

> I heard a shout, "Kill him! Kill him!" … They yelled in rage and urged each other to strike the first blow, but the Invisible One restrained them. At this dreadful moment a rushing and roaring sound came from the south. Every head instinctively turned, knowing it was one of their awful storms. As it came suddenly upon us, the mighty roaring of the wind and unceasing torrents awed my attackers into silence. Some began to withdraw from the scene. All lowered their weapons of war, and, terror-stricken, several exclaimed, "This is Jehovah's rain! Their Jehovah God is fighting for them and helping them. Run! Run!" A panic seized them as they threw away their torches and disappeared into the bush. I was left alone praising God for His marvelous works.[4]

Corrie ten Boom and her sister, Betsie, were sustained by prayer and a hidden Bible during their hideous ordeal at Ravensbruck, a German extermination camp in World War II. Even in the shadow of the crematorium, they knew they were in the care of "Him who was God even of Ravensbruck."[5] The sisters learned new dimensions of prayer, and Corrie realized, even after Betsie died, that "His timing is perfect. His will is our hiding place. Lord Jesus, keep me in Your will! Don't let me go mad by poking about outside it."[6]

I have been a learner in the school of prayer for many years, and God continues to teach me new insights about calling on Him.

I was flying in stormy weather in a small plane to speak at a retreat in South Texas. When we landed at College Station to refuel, authorities warned us that we should not fly farther south because of the storm's severity. The pilot ignored them. As we continued south, the ceiling got lower. Eight miles out of Lake Jackson, the tower radioed: "Turn back. We are fogged in. No one can land here." By now we were too low to bank and turn back. The pilot had no choice but to pull up into the "soup" and try to turn back. He would have to try it blind, without vision.

When the pilot felt that we were headed back north, he began to ease down to try to get below the lowest layer of clouds. I looked at the swirling mists and thought, *My all-powerful Lord controls those winds!* He was also all-present—right there in the grey tumbling clouds and with us in the little tossing plane. As we cleared the mistiness of the bottom layer, our plane zoomed beside a radio-broadcasting antenna, barely missing it!

By now we were lost. We began searching for a landmark, but we were flying in open country. Night came. We had no place to land, and no airport was expecting us. Then the pilot told me that he was not instrument-rated!

For the next hour we flew in the dark searching for a landing strip. I thought of the intercessors at Southcliff Baptist Church in Fort Worth who were praying for me. Much intercessory prayer depends on God's qualities of being all-knowing, all-powerful, and all-present. My heart eased at the thought.

Suddenly we spotted a landing field illuminated for cotton dusters. The pilot brought the plane to a safe landing. We had strayed 60 miles off course, and I missed the first session of the retreat. I knew, however, that my Lord had answered prayer mightily. Since that demonstration of His all-power, my prayer life has never been the same.[7]

Much intercessory prayer depends on God's qualities of being all-knowing, all-powerful, and all-present.

~~~~~~~~

You have been reading about other persons' experiences with prayer. What are some your own experiences? Complete the sentences on the following page.

1. To me, prayer is _____

_____

2. The best time of day for me to pray is _____

_____

3. My favorite place to pray is _____

_____

4. My most recent answer to prayer is _____

_____

5. My greatest answer to prayer was _____

_____

6. A prayer of mine that God has not yet answered is

_____

Spend a few minutes in prayer thanking God for His goodness and for the privilege of talking with Him.

Prayer knows no geographical, racial, or ethnic lines.

Universal in space. Prayer is universal not only in time but also in space. It knows no geographical, racial, or ethnic lines. The word *all* is one of the most important words in the Bible. The psalmist sang,

O Thou who dost hear prayer,
To Thee all men come (Ps. 65:2).

The "whoever believes" in John 3:16 is not restricted to one nationality. It is for everybody. Jesus is "the propitiation for our sins; and not for ours only, but also for those of the whole world" (1 John 2:2). And believers everywhere can talk with God.

Jesus declared, " 'I, if I be lifted up from the earth, will draw all men to Myself' " (John 12:32). Therefore, Paul could write in Romans 10:13, " 'Whoever will call upon the name of the Lord will be saved.' " In 1 Kings 8:41-43 Solomon prayed for the day when all people of the earth would know and fear the Lord. Psalm 86:9 predicts a universal worship of the one true God:

> All nations whom Thou hast made shall come and worship
>   before Thee, O Lord;
> And they shall glorify Thy name.

Yet many peoples of the world do not yet know our God. They cannot communicate with Him. They stumble on in darkness, trying in their misguided ways to achieve salvation. They do not know that God loves them and wants them to call on Him.

I have traveled in many lands on many continents, leading conferences for nationals and missionaries. The missionaries have shown me expressions of the local religion or religions they worked with. Many times I have visited Hindu, Buddhist, and Taoist temples; Shinto shrines; and Muslim mosques. I have seen animist emblems that dominated an area. I gradually began to realize that the fundamental difference between Christianity and all other religions is that Christianity alone is based on a personal relationship, expressed especially in personal love. In other religions I discovered superstitions, stringent laws, sometimes multiple gods, and even manipulation of the gods but not interaction with their gods on a consistent personal level. The element of personal love is strongly emphasized only in Christianity.[8]

The Great Commission commands us to tell the peoples of the world about Christ—that He can save them from their sins; that they can call on our Heavenly Father, who wants to hear from them; and that they can receive help from Him and enjoy His fellowship when they pray.

Prayer pervades the two great dimensions of time and space because God Himself is universal. He is in all dimensions, in all times, and in all places. He expects to meet people wherever they find themselves. The various manners of meeting with God become various kinds of prayer. The only conditions God places on the meeting time or the meeting place are those that bound and demonstrate His own character.

"Prayer is the easiest and hardest of all things; the simplest and the sublimest; the weakest and the most powerful; its results lie outside the range of human possibilities—they are limited only by the omnipotence of God."[9]
—E. M. Bounds, (1835–1913), Methodist pastor and itinerant preacher

Prayer Is Based on God's Nature

"The Lord is compassionate and gracious, Slow to anger and abounding in lovingkindness. He will not always strive with us; Nor will He keep His anger forever. He has not dealt with us according to our sins, Nor rewarded us according to our iniquities. For as high as the heavens are above the earth, So great is His lovingkindness toward those who fear Him. As far as the east is from the west, So far has He removed our transgressions from us" (Ps. 103:8-12).

Any address to a superior must be based on the character and position of that person. Therefore, prayer must be built on the foundation of the sovereignty and character of God. Jesus taught us to begin our prayers with an affirmation of the holiness of God's name (see Matt. 6:9). In most of the divine encounters in the Bible, the first attribute of God recognized by those who met Him was holiness. When Moses saw the burning bush on Mount Horeb, he heard a voice say, " 'Do not come near here; remove your sandals from your feet, for the place on which you are standing is holy ground' " (Ex. 3:5). When Isaiah saw the vision of God in the temple, the seraphim cried out, " 'Holy, Holy, Holy, is the Lord of hosts' " (Isa. 6:3). Daniel knew he could not pray apart from God's righteousness; in the famous prayer after his terrifying visions he acknowledged, " 'Righteousness belongs to Thee, O Lord' " (Dan. 9:7). When Peter recognized Jesus' awesome identity, he fell at Jesus' feet and cried out, " 'Depart from me, for I am a sinful man, O Lord!' " (Luke 5:8).

But the seemingly opposite side of God's character is His mercy toward sinners. James described Him as being compassionate and merciful (see Jas. 5:11). Many of the psalms (see Pss. 86:15; 145:8) lyrically sing of this attracting aspect of God's nature. Psalm 103:8-12 describes the extent to which God will forgive sins. Take a moment to read those thrilling verses in the margin.

God's awesome holiness seems to separate Him from sinful people, but His tenderness for His creatures draws Him close to us. It seems illogical that a God so terrifyingly holy could also be so "plenteous in mercy" (Ps. 103:8, KJV). Yet this verse implies that the Lord is wealthy in mercy!

Following a conference in Ohio, a man asked me a difficult question: "In the Old Testament God is so terrifyingly holy that He seems distant. But in the New Testament God is so warm and loving that He seems to be trying to get close to us. Those seem to be opposite pictures. Can those two opposites be reconciled?"

Yes, they can. God is infinite and unchanging. Because our human minds cannot comprehend infinity, God reveals to us various aspects of His nature. Sometimes these aspects appear to be opposites. We cannot begin to understand God's nature without accepting that He can have holiness and love at once. God's holi-

16

ness is a wonderful and yet a dreadful fact. In our sinful human condition we find His holiness an alarming attribute. However, God is love, and "God so loved the world" (John 3:16). God took great pains to reach us with His love. God's love is also a fact. Holiness causes us to fear God, while His compassion and love draw us close. These attributes exist in the same magnificent Person.

The clearest example of God's holiness and love is what God did at Calvary. Nothing shows us God's holiness like Calvary. Because of sin, nothing less than Christ's shed blood on the cross could satisfy the requirements of God's awesome holiness. At the same time, nothing like Christ's sacrifice shows us how great God's love is. The cross shows us how far God was willing to go to reach us in His infinite love.

We risk irreverence and loss of perspective if we do not acknowledge God's holiness. We also miss God Himself if we fail to see the immense love revealed through the Person of Jesus Christ. Both God's holiness and His love were best demonstrated in Christ's crucifixion and death on the cross.[10]

It is unmistakably certain in the Bible that God is infinitely holy and at the same time compassionate toward sinful people. This paradox, like many other Bible paradoxes, gives our finite minds God's way of enclosing infinity. Although we can never fully understand this paradox, it contains the truth about the nature of God.

Prayer can have no meaning unless it takes into account God's total nature. He is holy; we come to Him on those grounds. He is love; we pray knowing that He is concerned about our needs. Because He is merciful, God understands and cares about human need. In most of the prayers of biblical characters, God took the initiative. That initiating God tells us: " 'Ask, and it shall be given to you; seek, and you shall find; knock, and it shall be opened to you. For everyone who asks receives, and he who seeks finds, and to him who knocks it shall be opened' " (Matt. 7:7-8).

The greatest saints have always known intuitively, from the depths of their spiritual nature, that God desires to provide for His own. Abraham assured Isaac as he was preparing to ascend Mount Moriah, " 'God will provide for Himself the lamb for the burnt offering' " (Gen. 22:8). Only one who grasped the truth that God is concerned about human need could cry out, "The

"Between the humble and contrite heart and the majesty of heaven there are no barriers: The only password is prayer."[11]
—Matthew Henry (1662–1714), English pastor and Scripture commentator

Lord is my shepherd" (Ps. 23:1) or "The Lord is your keeper" (Ps. 121:5). Supremely, it is Jesus who assures us with the most graphic pictures that God is deeply concerned for our needs. He asked, as though it were the most reasonable question imaginable, " 'If God so arrays the grass of the field, which is alive today and tomorrow is thrown into the furnace, will He not much more do so for you, O men of little faith?' " (Matt. 6:30).

God has chosen to relate Himself to us as a loving Father.

God has chosen to relate Himself to us as a loving Father. Jesus told us to address Him as "our Father" (Matt. 6:9). Only a divine Father would want to number our hairs (see Matt. 10:30)! Jesus asked a question in Matthew 7:11 that is really a logical affirmation: " 'If you then, being evil, know how to give good gifts to your children, how much more shall your Father who is in heaven give what is good to those who ask Him!' "

And it is not only as Father that God demonstrates His infinite concern. The Bible provides us with other characterizations of God that bring Him close. He is also shepherd (see Ps. 23:1) and keeper (see Ps. 121:5). He is our

refuge and strength,
A very present help in trouble (Ps. 46:1).

God is a sun and shield (see Ps. 84:11). Christ established God's nearness in even more intimate terms. If He is brother (see Heb. 2:11), we are His brother or sister. If He is teacher (see John 3:2), we are His disciples. If He is the vine, we are His own branches (see John 15:5). He almost exhausts language to clarify for us how caring He is and how intimate with us He wants to be.

Describe a time in your life when you were especially aware of God's caring for you.

_____

_____

_____

Prayer Is Effective

God obviously hears all things, and yet He says He hears the prayers of His children in a special way. How can someone say to an all-hearing God,

"Thou art my God;
Give ear, O Lord, to the voice of my supplications" (Ps. 140:6)?

Sometimes the word *hear* in Hebrew carries the idea of *respond to*, as in Zechariah 10:6: " 'I am the Lord their God, and I will answer [*King James,* hear] them.' " The certainty of God's hearing is established by Psalm 116:1-2:

I love the Lord, because He hears
My voice and my supplications.
Because He has inclined His ear to me,
Therefore I shall call upon Him as long as I live.

The word for *hears* in Psalm 116:1 is the same as in Zechariah 10:6—God hears, answers, or responds to. God hears us when we pray.

Prayer is effective because God relates to human need. Because God is personal, He relates to human need in a personal way. Again and again, we find persons appealing to God as a Person. Exodus 33:13-14 records a remarkably personal dialogue between Moses and God. Moses pleaded, " 'I pray Thee, if I have found favor in Thy sight, let me know Thy ways, that I may know Thee, so that I may find favor in Thy sight.' " God answered, " 'My presence shall go with you, and I will give you rest.' " David's plea for forgiveness in Psalm 51 would have no meaning if it were not poignantly personal:

Do not cast me away from Thy presence,
And do not take Thy Holy Spirit from me (Ps. 51:11).

The joy of God's personal presence is rapturously described in Psalm 16:11:

In Thy presence is fulness of joy;
In Thy right hand there are pleasures forever.

Because God is personal, He relates to human need in a personal way.

Fellowship is a mark of personhood. God is actively seeking fellowship with persons whose hearts are like His. Hanani the seer told King Asa that " 'the eyes of the Lord move to and fro throughout the earth that He may strongly support those whose heart is completely His' " (2 Chron. 16:9). Peter made Psalm 34:15 a part of the New Testament message:

"The eyes of the Lord are upon the righteous,
And His ears attend to their prayer" (1 Pet. 3:12).

> *"Prayer is not conquering God's reluctance, but taking hold upon God's willingness."*[12]
> —Phillips Brooks, (1835–93), pastor of Trinity Church; Boston, Massachusetts

Friendship is a mark of personhood. What do people do in personal fellowship? They talk, walk, and share. Bible history is replete with individuals who enjoyed an intimate relationship with God. We are told that Enoch "walked with God three hundred years" (Gen. 5:22) and also that Noah "walked with God" (Gen. 6:9). In Isaiah 41:8 God called Abraham His friend. James 2:23 makes clear that Abraham's faith, not his performance, earned him this title: "The Scripture was fulfilled which says, 'And Abraham believed God, and it was reckoned to him as righteousness,' and he was called the friend of God."

God hears an individual's prayer. The psalmist expressed gratitude for answers in the past. He wrote,

In my distress I called upon the Lord,
And cried to my God for help;
He heard my voice out of His temple,
And my cry for help before Him came into His ears (Ps. 18:6).

He also expressed confidence in future answers:

My voice rises to God, and I will cry aloud;
My voice rises to God, and He will hear me (Ps. 77:1).

A Christian is assured that through Christ we "have our access in one Spirit to the Father" (Eph. 2:18).

Prayer was effective in the Old Testament. The Old Testament preserves beautiful instances of answers to the prayers of individuals. On the backside of the desert an old man stood before a burning bush (see Ex. 3:1-5). Receiving his call and commission from God, Moses returned to Egypt, the rod of God in his hand (see Ex. 4:20), to deliver the greatest emancipation proclamation in history (see Ex. 5:1). The great deliverance of God's people from slavery was wrought through prayer (see Ex. 5—14).

The Israelites journeyed toward the promised land, protected and provided for through the prayers of Moses. Through prayer the bitter waters of Marah became clear and sweet (see Ex. 15:22-25). Prayer brought down bread from heaven, six days a week, for their long journey (see Ex. 16). Prayer brought water from a rock (see Ex. 17:1-7). Prayer enabled Joshua to defeat the Amalekites as Moses stood on a hill making intercession (see Ex. 17:8-13).

Prayer brought down the formidable walls of Jericho (see Josh. 6). Prayer stopped the sun and moon over the valley of Ajalon while Joshua battled the Amorites (see Josh. 10:1-15).

During the long, dark period of the judges, prayer delivered the children of Israel many times from their enemies when they turned to God following periods of moral decline and apostasy (see Judg. 3:9; 4:3; 6:7; 10:10).

When prayer opened the womb of a childless woman named Hannah (see 1 Sam. 1:11), she named her newborn son " 'asked him of the Lord,' " or Samuel (see 1 Sam. 1:20). Later, that young boy answered God's call and became the great prophet and judge of the people (see 1 Sam. 3).

Prayer enabled the prophet Elijah to wear the keys to the clouds on his belt. He prayed, and there was no rain for 3½ years (see 1 Kings 17:1; Jas. 5:17). Prayer kept meal in a barrel and oil in a vessel during the prophet's stay in Sidon (see 1 Kings 17:9-16). Prayer raised the dead son of the widow who owned the meal barrel and oil vessel (see 1 Kings 17:17-24). Prayer brought fire from heaven to consume Elijah's sacrifice on Carmel (see 1 Kings 18:37).

During the time of godly king Hezekiah, prayer brought one angel from heaven to slay 185,000 Assyrian soldiers and lift a siege from Jerusalem (see 2 Kings 19:14-35). Prayer added 15 years to Hezekiah's life (see 2 Kings 20:1-6).

Prayer enabled Nehemiah and his workers to rebuild the wall around Jerusalem in 52 days (see Neh. 6:1-15). Prayer gave Esther courage to risk her life in approaching the king (see Esth. 4:16).

Prayer gave the hungry lions lockjaw and granted Daniel a night of rest in the lions' den (see Dan. 6:10-22). Prayer gave the prophet Daniel the vision to look across the centuries and see the coming of the Messiah (see Dan. 9:3-27).

The great deliverance of God's people from slavery was wrought through prayer.

"Prayer is the key that unlocks all the storehouses of God's infinite grace and power."[13]
—R. A. Torrey (1856–1928), evangelist and pastor

Prayer was effective in the New Testament. The New Testament furnishes us with moving examples of answered prayers in the early church. After Jesus' ascension the apostles "were continually devoting themselves to prayer" (Acts 1:14). This continual prayer brought the Holy Spirit on the day of Pentecost (see Acts 2:1-4). As a result, Peter, who had cursed and denied Christ a few weeks earlier, was empowered to preach with such boldness and power that three thousand people were saved (see Acts 2:41). Prayer shook the building where the early Christians prayed and gave them boldness to preach (see Acts 4:29-31). When Tabitha the seamstress died, Peter prayed, and she came to life again (see Acts 9:40). Prayer brought down a sheet from heaven filled with all kinds of animals to teach Peter and the early church that God does not show favoritism but that all persons everywhere, whatever race or ethnic background, may come to Christ (see Acts 10:9-16). Prayer brought an angel to free Peter from a death-row prison cell (see Acts 12:1-10). Prayer empowered Paul and his companions to win people to Christ and to plant churches across the Roman Empire (see Acts 13:3; 16:25; 2 Cor. 1:11; Eph. 1:15-19; 6:18-21; Col. 1:9-12).

Match the following prayers with the persons who prayed them. You may need to use a concordance to find some of these. Watch out! Some names are used more than once, and some are not used at all.

___ 1. "Father, forgive them; for they do not know what they are doing."

___ 2. "Jesus, Son of David, have mercy on me!"

___ 3. "Wash me thoroughly from my iniquity, and cleanse me from my sin. ... Against Thee, Thee only, I have sinned."

___ 4. "There is no one holy like the Lord, indeed, there is no one besides Thee, nor is there any rock like our God."

a. Moses
b. Hannah
c. David
d. Isaiah
e. Jesus
f. John
g. Peter
h. Centurion
i. Bartimaeus
j. Stephen
k. Paul

___ 5. "I do not ask Thee to take them
out of the world, but to keep them
from the evil one."

___ 6. "If Thou wilt, forgive their sin—
and if not, please blot me out from
Thy book which Thou hast written!"

___ 7. "Lord, do not hold this sin
against them!"

___ 8. "Depart from me, for I am a
sinful man."

___ 9. "Father, if it is possible, let this cup
pass from Me; yet not as I will,
but as Thou wilt."

___ 10. "Blessed be the God and Father
of our Lord Jesus Christ, who has
blessed us with every spiritual blessing."

___ 11. "O Lord my God, in Thee I have
taken refuge; save me from all those
who pursue me, and deliver me."

Prayer has been effective throughout Christian history.
Examples of God's hearing and answering prayers can be found
not only in the Bible but also throughout Christian history. The
modern missions movement was born in prayer. In the mid-1700s
pastors in Scotland began praying for revival. Prayer meetings
spread in Scotland, England, Wales, Ireland, and North America,
and revival came. From this prayer movement the cobbler William
Carey was saved and was called to preach. In 1793 he left for India
as a missionary. Accounts of missionaries like Carey, John Paton,
Adoniram and Ann Judson, Hudson Taylor, David Brainerd,
Robert and Mary Moffat, David Livingston, Robert Morrison,
Jonathan Goforth, Lottie Moon, Amy Carmichael, John "Praying"
Hyde, Gladys Aylward, Bill Wallace, William Cameron Townsend,
Joy Ridderhof, Jim Elliott, and Nate Saint teach us that God hears
and answers prayer.

George Müller operated a large orphanage in Bristol, England,
on prayer and faith. For years God miraculously met every need,
sometimes moments before the money was needed for a bill. His
journal documents thousands of answers to his prayers.[14] Charles
Haddon Spurgeon was a great pastor in London in the 1800s.

The modern missions movement was born in prayer.

Thousands came to hear him preach, and even today dozens of volumes of his messages are still in print and are widely circulated. Many people who have heard of Spurgeon's powerful preaching do not know that beneath the auditorium where Spurgeon preached each Sunday, a small group of Christians met and continuously prayed for their pastor as he preached.[15]

Prayer is effective today. God also answers our prayers today. My life has been immeasurably enriched by a growing awareness each day that God's children are special to Him and that He hears us when we pray. Some of the greatest prayer lessons I have learned have been in the crucible of sickness and suffering in my family. My wife, Laverne, was diagnosed with cancer in 1983 and had surgery and chemotherapy. Treatment was not as advanced then as it is now; the oncologist gave her a 50-50 chance of survival. When I first heard that dreaded word *cancer,* I had the same reaction most men do when faced with the awful brutality of the possibly terminal illness of their wives. There came the horror of the finality of death. All these thoughts were below the level of my conscious mind. When they surfaced, I would not give them voice, although my conscious mind was aware of the ugly facts our fallen race has to deal with. I was horrified and very frightened—terrified at the idea of losing my life companion. The finality of that loss was a bottomless pit I could not face.

God gently led Laverne and me to study together that profound book on suffering, 2 Corinthians. I canceled all my engagements during her chemotherapy. Each evening after dinner she and I would sit down together with our notebooks and Bibles in hand. We worked our way along very carefully, word by word, phrase by phrase, verse by verse. As we studied and prayed together, we began to sense the leadership of the Holy Spirit bringing new insights—and importantly, the ability to appropriate the indescribable comforts that God's Spirit can give during suffering. A new glory entered our relationship with one another and especially with the Lord who was enlightening His Word.

The turning point came when we began to comprehend the enormous significance of chapter 3, verse 18: "We all, with unveiled face beholding as in a mirror the glory of the Lord, are being transformed into the same image from glory to glory, just as from the Lord, the Spirit." Yes, the suffering was still there. Yes, the dismal prospects of nausea, weakness, baldness, and death still

> *Some of the greatest prayer lessons have been learned in the crucible of sickness and suffering.*

threatened. Yet now we entered a new glory with God's own Spirit each night as we studied together. The unhappy aspects of our plight no longer intimidated us so much; we somehow understood the comfort of the Holy Comforter on a scale we had never known before. We had a oneness in our marriage that was new and different.

When we reached the end of chemotherapy, Laverne declared that if she had the choice of not having cancer and therefore not learning what we had learned or of having cancer with the new glories we now knew, she would prefer the latter. And I actually agree with her! The awfulness of the realities was still there, but we had somehow achieved a new glory in our relationship with one another. We had discovered that the spiritual glories we gained through new insights and the comfort of the Holy Comforter are far greater than any physical comfort. Yet we did not know at the time that God would be taking us far, far deeper into an understanding of His purposes when our daughter later developed cancer. We were destined to go through another time of suffering and crying out to God.[16]

Our daughter, Melana, was diagnosed with cancer in 1999 at the age of 42. Steve and Melana had been married at that time for 22 years and had six children. The cancer was a large, aggressive mass, and we later learned that her lymph nodes were extensively involved. The news devastated all of us and drove us to our knees in a new way. Melana went through three months of chemotherapy, a mastectomy, five more months of chemotherapy, another mastectomy, and six weeks of radiation. All of us began living even more closely in Scripture and praying as never before. Melana and I began memorizing more Scripture. She and I began comparing notes of what we believed God was teaching us through that experience, and we finally realized that the Holy Spirit was leading us both in the same direction—to view all of life from God's perspective. We began thinking more in terms of eternity rather than the confines of our world.

Our family had always had times of prayer, individually and collectively. But this new cancer brought us up sharp against the urgency of an even more constant contact with God. Before we would have claimed a healthy, regular prayer life. In our new desperation, pain and urgency made us realize that our prayer life had been at times sporadic (although we prayed every day), at times

"Hear ye the Master: 'Him that cometh to me I will in no wise cast out.' Come on, mothers with your babies! Come, blind Bartimeus! Come, thou prodigal! Come, Zaccheus and Matthew! Come, ye Magdalenes! Come, dying thieves! The door is wide open by day and night. No sentinel blocks the way. … Come yourself to God Himself."[17] —B. H. Carroll (1843– 1914), founder and first president of Southwestern Baptist Theological Seminary

inattentive and distracted, and often inept or embarrassed. Occasionally, we contented ourselves with surface-level praying ("God bless the missionaries," "bless this food," "be with so-and-so").

Now our family needed to know how God felt about us while we were in the act of praying—all the time. From that need itself, God led us to a new level of prayer—a level that constitutes one of the most challenging aspects of heaven's view: God pays unremitting, close attention to each of us, not only when we are aware of Him or need Him but also when we do not even realize how dependent we are on Him.

My and Melana's former ineptness or discomfort in prayer usually expressed itself after we failed to "stay with Him"—and sin or worldly attitudes crept in without our conscious awareness. Our desperation made us realize that regardless of circumstances God keeps His word that He will never leave us (see Heb. 13:5). Once we became conscious of that, we could not ignore His helping presence. Heaven concentrates on us, and now we learned that we can also be instant with God continually. We do not return to God—we never leave Him![18]

My family and I do not know what the future holds, but we know experientially the truth of Hebrews 13:5-6: "[God] has said,

'I will never desert you,
nor will I ever forsake you.'

So that we confidently say,

'The Lord is my helper, I will not be afraid
What can man do to me?' "

Prayer is the shaping force of history.

History and personal experience, then, demonstrate that although God is sovereign, He desires the fellowship of those He has created. Prayer grows from God's own nature and from His plans for us. His plans involve all people, so all may come to Him, and He delights to hear them when they pray. Prayer is the shaping force of history. God used Moses' prayers to preserve Israel through the wandering years. He used Nehemiah's prayer to make possible the rebuilding of the wall around Jerusalem. Jesus' prayers shaped His disciples and helped develop them into the kind of people who would populate a new kind of kingdom. Paul's prayers were God's instrument for shaping the personality and destiny of the new church as it spread across the Mediterranean world. In the Bible, prayer is the amazing cooperation of humankind in bringing God's plans for this world to fruition. Although God could move unilaterally because He is sovereign, His wisdom allows persons to share with Him His own divine work. An important part of that divine work is done through prayer.

Dr. Hunt writes, "Prayer is the shaping force of history." Do you agree or disagree with this statement?
❏ **Agree** ❏ **Disagree**

How could you explain the statement in view of the reality of terrorism, poverty, and war?

_____

_____

_____

_____

_____

List examples from biblical history that substantiate the statement.

_____

_____

_____

_____

Sweet hour of prayer,
* sweet hour of prayer,*
That calls me from
* a world of care*
And bids me at my
* Father's throne*
Make all my wants
* and wishes known!*

In seasons of distress
* and grief,*
My soul has often found
* relief,*
And oft escaped
* the tempter's snare*
By Thy return, sweet hour
* of prayer.*[19]

[1]Herbert Lockyer, *All the Prayers of the Bible* (Grand Rapids: Zondervan, 1959), 171.

[2]Spiros Zodhiates, ed., *Hebrew-Greek Key Study Bible* (Chattanooga: AMG Publishers, 1991), 1657.

[3]George W. Truett, *Follow Thou Me* (Nashville: Broadman Press, n.d.), 10.

[4]Benjamin Unseth, *John Paton* (Minneapolis: Bethany House, 1996), 104-5.

[5]Corrie ten Boom with John and Elizabeth Sherrill, *The Hiding Place* (Washington Depot, CT: Chosen Books, 1971), 176.

[6]Ibid., 203.

[7]T.W. Hunt and Catherine Walker, *Disciple's Prayer Life* (Nashville: LifeWay Press, 1997), 21.

[8]Adapted from T. W. Hunt and Melana Hunt Monroe, *From Heaven's View* (Nashville: LifeWay Press, 2002).

[9]E. M. Bounds, *The Complete Works of E. M. Bounds on Prayer* (Grand Rapids: Baker Books, 1990), 317.

[10]Adapted from T.W. Hunt and Claude V. King, *The Mind of Christ* (Nashville: LifeWay Press, 1997), 155–56.

[11]Matthew Henry, in *All the Promises of the Bible* by Herbert Lockyer (Grand Rapids: Zondervan, 1962), 147.

[12]Phillips Brooks, in Lockyer, *All the Promises,* 147.

[13]R. A. Torrey, *The Power of Prayer* (New York: Fleming H. Revell, 1924), 17.

[14]A. T. Pierson, *George Müller of Bristol* (Grand Rapids: Kregel Publications, 1999).

[15]T. W. Hunt and Claude V. King, *In God's Presence* (Nashville: LifeWay Press, 1995), 7.

[16]Adapted from Hunt and Monroe, *From Heaven's View.*

[17]B. H. Carroll, *Messages on Prayer* (Nashville: Broadman Press, 1942), 26.

[18]Adapted from Hunt and Monroe, *From Heaven's View.*

[19]William Walford, "Sweet Hour of Prayer," in *The Baptist Hymnal,* 445.

Answers to matching activity on pages 22–23: 1. e, 2. i, 3. c, 4. b, 5. e, 6. a, 7. j, 8. g, 9. e, 10. k, 11. f

Chapter 2
Our Example and
Our Helper in Prayer

Jesus, Our Example in Prayer

Jesus was a man of prayer. The earliest utterance recorded from Jesus' lips (see Luke 2:49) occurred in what He later called a house of prayer. Isaiah had so named it (see Isa. 56:7), and no doubt that function—prayer—was important in Jesus' own view of the temple. It was His Father's house (see John 2:16), and His outrage toward the money changers was that an activity so foreign to the spirit of prayer should find a place in the temple.

The writer of Hebrews vividly pictured Jesus' prayers: "In the days of His flesh, He offered up both prayers and supplications with loud crying and tears to the One able to save Him from death, and He was heard because of His piety" (Heb. 5:7). The translators of the *New American Standard Bible* infer from the verb form in Luke 5:16 that Jesus' withdrawals for prayer were continual: "He Himself would often slip away to the wilderness and pray."

Jesus' life was singular in His emphasis on prayer. Having emptied Himself of His prerogatives as God (see Phil. 2:6), He functioned as other human beings must function—through prayer. His power derived from prayer (see Mark 9:29). On at least 11 different occasions Jesus taught on prayer, beginning in the early part of His Galilean ministry, in the Sermon on the Mount, and continuing throughout His life. The night before Jesus died, He was still practicing prayer and teaching on it. His example and His teaching are the greatest encouragement in the Bible for us to pray.

Jesus Prayed Continually
The occasions for Jesus' prayers were many and varied. He prayed in the early morning (see Mark 1:35) and at night (see Matt. 14:23). He often prayed alone. This must have impressed John, who piled up phrases to intensify the solitariness of some of Jesus'

"Very early in the morning, while it was still dark He got up, went out, and made His way to a deserted place. And He was praying there" *(Mark 1:35).*

29

prayers. He "withdrew again to the mountain by Himself alone" (John 6:15). Any of the three expressions—"withdrew," "by Himself," and "alone"—would have indicated seclusion; yet John felt compelled to provide all three. Jesus prayed with others present (see Matt. 11:25-26), and He prayed in large public gatherings (see Matt. 14:19). Luke tells us that He prayed all night (see Luke 6:12).

Sometimes Jesus is pictured as praying during one of His miracles (see John 11:41-42). On four different occasions He is described as blessing a meal (see Matt. 15:36; 26:26-27; Luke 9:16; 24:30). Twice He blessed people: He blessed the children who were brought to Him (see Matt. 19:13-15), and He blessed His disciples as He parted from them at His ascension (see Luke 24:50).

Major decisions in Jesus' life were preceded by prayer. Since "the Spirit impelled Him" (Mark 1:12) into the wilderness for the temptation by Satan, it is likely that Jesus was in a state of prayer after His baptism. His decision to leave Capernaum and preach in "the other cities also" followed His prayer in "a lonely place" (Mark 1:35; Luke 4:42-43). One of the most significant decisions of His life, the choosing of the twelve apostles, came after a night of prayer (see Luke 6:12-13). Evidently, Jesus could have chosen His disciples from a number of people, for "He called His disciples to Him; and chose twelve of them." Therefore, He must have prayed about many people before He chose the twelve.

The great personal crises of Jesus' life were intense moments of prayer.

Supremely, the great personal crises of Jesus' life were intense moments of prayer. In Gethsemane He fell on His face (see Matt. 26:39) and addressed God with the intimate title Abba (see Mark 14:36). Mark and Luke simply reported His agonizing request that the cup be taken from Him, along with His commitment to God's will. Matthew recorded that the second and third prayers specifically detailed His determination to carry out God's will: " 'My Father, if this cannot pass away unless I drink it, Thy will be done' " (Matt. 26:42). The final utterance of His life was also a commitment in prayer: " 'Father, into Thy hands I commit My spirit' " (Luke 23:46). The importance of these prayers cannot be overstated. They were part of events that have significance for all of us.

❦

Read the following statements about Jesus' prayer life. Which statements are true? Which are false? Write a *T* or an *F* in the blank beside each statement.

___ 1. Jesus often prayed early in the morning.

___ 2. There is no record of Jesus praying in public.

___ 3. Jesus chose His disciples after praying all night.

___ 4. Other than beside the grave of Lazarus, the New Testament does not record Jesus weeping.

___ 5. Jesus often slipped away and went to the wilderness to pray.

___ 6. Jesus prayed as our example, not because He had a personal need to pray.

___ 7. When Jesus prayed in Gethsemane, He expressed an unwillingness to die on the cross.

___ 8. The final recorded words of Jesus before He died were words of prayer.

The most sublime and noble prayer in the Bible is Christ's High-Priestly prayer in John 17. It speaks of Christ's eternal redemptive work and His relationship with the Father. It also contains petitions to the Father that are important to all people. These various factors demonstrate an interworking that is remarkable in its unity. The opening five verses record Jesus' prayer for Himself; the rest of the prayer is on behalf of His disciples and those who would follow Him through the centuries.

Jesus' prayer for Himself can be summed up in verse 5: " 'Now, glorify Thou Me together with Thyself, Father, with the glory which I had with Thee before the world was.' " Here Christ prayed for the restoration of the right order of things that had existed from all eternity. The work of redemption should properly be climaxed by His lordship over all creation and His headship over the church. Rainsford sums it up: "He asks His Father to take the Son of Man into the position He as the Son of God occupied before His incarnation; that there, as the Representative of His people, and as Head of His Church, and Head over all things to His Church, He might rule everything in heaven, and earth, and hell, for their benefit. The prayer means nothing less than that; God only knows how much more it means."[1]

The Lord's petitions on behalf of His disciples reveal a parallel between His sense of identity with the Father (see vv. 6-12) and the identity of His disciples with Himself (vv. 12-22). This paralleling of relationships serves as the background and basis for His requests on behalf of His disciples.

The most sublime and noble prayer in the Bible is Christ's High-Priestly prayer in John 17.

Jesus' identity with His Father. Jesus' first identity with the Father is at the point of the divine glory: " 'Glorify Thy Son, that the Son may glorify Thee' " (v. 1); " 'glorify Thou Me together with Thyself' " (v. 5). From any other lips such a prayer would be blasphemy; from Christ, it is a self-identity with the Father's deity. Jesus claimed the name of the Father: " 'Keep them in Thy name, the name which Thou hast given Me' " (v. 11). His disciples were first those of His Father: " 'Thine they were, and Thou gavest them to Me' " (v. 6). He identified with His Father in their common possessions: " 'All things that are Mine are Thine, and Thine are Mine' " (v. 10). The work of the Father and the Son was also identical. After asking the Father to keep them in the Father's name, He said this keeping would be a continuation of His own work: " 'While I was with them, I was keeping them in Thy name' " (v. 12). Christ identified with the Father in a common glory, a common name, common disciples, common possessions, and a common work. He identified with the Father's deity and shared His glory.

Jesus' identity with His disciples. Jesus identified with His disciples' humanity. Their joy was the same as His joy: " 'These things I speak in the world, that they may have My joy made full in themselves' " (v. 13). His disciples were not of the world, even as He was not of the world (see v. 16). The mission of Christ and His disciples was identical: " 'As Thou didst send Me into the world, I also have sent them into the world' " (v. 18). He identified their sanctification with His: " 'For their sakes I sanctify Myself, that they themselves also may be sanctified in truth' " (v. 19). He even shared His glory with the disciples: " 'The glory which Thou hast given Me I have given to them' " (v. 22). Christ identified with His disciples in a common joy, a common separation, a common mission, a common sanctification, and a common glory. A progression is evident from joy to glory.

Having established the reality of His relationship with His Father and His followers, Jesus interwove five specific petitions for the disciples.

1. "Holy Father, keep them in Thy name" (v. 11), more specifically stated in verse 15, "Keep them from the evil one."
2. "Sanctify them in the truth" (v. 17).
3. "… that they also may be in Us" (v. 21).
4. "Father, I desire that they also, whom Thou hast given Me, be with Me where I am" (v. 24).

5. "… that they may all be one" (v. 21, repeated as concomitants of other facts in vv. 11,22-23).

《◦◦◦◦》

Read Jesus' prayer in John 17. List His intercessions that apply to Christians today.

_____

_____

Other statements in the prayer are actually consequences of Jesus' statements or requests. If we are one in the Father and the Son, the world will believe that the Father sent the Son (see v. 21). If we are perfected in unity, the world will know that the Father sent the Son and that the Father loved the disciples as He loves the Son (see v. 23). The fact that Christ makes the Father's name known will cause the Father's love to be in the disciples (see v. 26). These are not requests but prayerful recognitions of the right order of things. They are important because they are the clearest specimen we have of Christ's prayer as High Priest.

This was not the only occasion when Christ prayed for others; see, for example, His prayer for Peter in Luke 22.32. But it is extremely instructive. John 17 is the longest of Christ's recorded prayers. It exhibits a profound sense of self-identity; provides a divine basis for God the Father to answer the prayers; and, in view of its occasion (the night before He gave His life), demonstrates the most powerful faith of all the prayers of the Bible.

John 17 demonstrates the most powerful faith of all the prayers of the Bible.

《◦◦◦◦》

George Newton (1602–81), a Puritan pastor in England, said in a sermon on John 17, "Our prayers shew our hearts to Christ; his prayer shews his heart to us."[3] Meditate on the statement and complete the following.

Explain what you think Newton meant.

_____

_____

Based on the prayer Jesus prayed in John 17, how would you describe His heart?

_____

_____

_____

Now consider the first part of Newton's statement: "Our prayers show our hearts to Christ." Based on your prayer life this past week, how would you describe your heart as Jesus sees it?

_____

_____

Are there differences between His heart and your heart? Spend a few minutes praying that your heart will become more like His heart.

Jesus Taught His Followers to Pray

Most New Testament Letters include teachings on prayer, but the most extensive statements of prayer principles are those of Jesus. Jesus' most detailed statement of His training program for His disciples is the Sermon on the Mount (Matt. 5—7). A significant portion of that program is devoted to His teachings on prayer.

Two prohibitions. Jesus first told His disciples how not to pray (see Matt. 6:5-8), and then He gave a model of the directions prayer should take (see Matt. 6:9-14). The negative teaching included two strong prohibitions that contrast a disciple's prayer with false prayer. A disciple is not to pray like religious hypocrites—for display—and a disciple is not to pray like pagans—babbling meaninglessly.

In the command to avoid display, Jesus demonstrated His high regard for the holy. His own example commended His emphasis on privacy. Later, He would warn about the scribes, who " 'for appearance' sake offer long [public] prayers' " (Mark 12:40). Jesus' command to His disciples was " 'When thou prayest, thou shalt

A disciple is not to pray like religious hypocrites— for display.

not be as the hypocrites' " (Matt. 6:5, KJV). His emphasis on privacy is underlined by the singular pronoun. He further emphasized the importance of privacy by stating the command in a positive form: the individual is to go into an inner room; shut out the world; and pray to the Father, who is in secret (see Matt. 6:6).

The second negative command, like the rest of Jesus' teachings on prayer, is given in the plural and has general application: we are not to use " 'meaningless repetition' " (Matt. 6:7), or to babble endlessly. This does not prohibit long prayers, for Jesus prayed all night (see Luke 6:12). Every recorded example of lengthy prayer by Jesus was in private. The command to avoid babbling is a reminder that God does not need information and prefers that our prayers be to the point. The disciples would have been aware of the hours-long wail of the priests of Baal in their contest with Elijah on Mount Carmel (see 1 Kings 18:26), in sharp contrast to Elijah's brief, to-the-point prayer to the Lord (see 1 Kings 18:36-37).

Prayers of faith. Jesus repeatedly emphasized the importance of faith in our prayers. At the foot of the Mount of Transfiguration, when the disciples failed to cast out a demon, He told them, " 'If you have faith as a mustard seed, you shall say to this mountain, "Move from here to there," and it shall move; and nothing shall be impossible to you' " (Matt. 17:20). He repeated this illustration when the disciples were amazed by the withering of a fig tree He had cursed: " 'Truly I say to you, if you have faith, and do not doubt, you shall not only do what was done to the fig tree, but even if you say to this mountain, "Be taken up and cast into the sea," it shall happen. And all things you ask in prayer, believing, you shall receive' " (Matt. 21:21-22).

The Model Prayer. The Model Prayer, or the disciples' prayer, teaches us to address God as our Father. In His teaching on prayer Jesus repeatedly referred to God as " 'your Father' " (Matt. 6:6,15). In the Synoptic Gospels (Matthew, Mark, and Luke) God is often called " 'your heavenly Father' " (Matt. 6:14; Luke 11:13) or " 'your Father who is in heaven' " (Matt. 7:11; Mark 11:26). In John God is usually " 'the Father' " (John 14:13; 15:16; 16:23,26-27). Jesus introduced us to an intimate relationship with God to a degree that had not been emphasized up to His time.

In the Model Prayer content and order are important. The prayer includes six petitions, divided into two equal parts. The first three are concerned with God's nature and purposes. We are to

Jesus repeatedly emphasized the importance of faith in our prayers.

pray on behalf of the holiness of God's name, the primacy of His sovereignty, and the accomplishment of His purposes on earth:

> *"Hallowed be Thy name.*
> *Thy kingdom come.*
> *Thy will be done,*
> *On earth as it is in heaven" (Matt. 6:9-10).*

The second group of petitions is made on behalf of the petitioners. One petition requests the supplying of physical needs—sustenance. The other two petitions are made for the supplying of spiritual needs—the restoration of fellowship with God through forgiveness and the maintenance of fellowship through protection from temptation.

> *"Give us this day our daily bread.*
> *And forgive us our debts, as we also have forgiven our debtors.*
> *And do not lead us into temptation, but deliver us from evil"*
> *(Matt. 6:11-13).*

In the prayer for forgiveness Christ made it plain that forgiveness is possible for us because our willingness to forgive identifies us with God in His forgiving character. Later, in Gethsemane He would amplify and emphasize the prayer for deliverance from temptation by admonishing the disciples to " 'keep watching and praying, that you may not enter into temptation' " (Matt. 26:41). In the latter passage Christ made it clear that even a willing spirit can succumb to the weakness of the flesh. The only way to overcome the flesh is to be constantly vigilant in prayer.

Other teachings on prayer. Jesus assured His followers of God's goodness to hear and answer prayer. He told us that the human actions of asking, seeking, and knocking would be met with such divine response that we in turn will receive, find, and face an open door (see Matt. 7:7-8). God's nature is such that asking elicits His giving, seeking obtains His guidance, and knocking reveals a divinely opened opportunity. Many times in His teachings on prayer Jesus used the word *ask*. He assured us that our Heavenly Father knows better how to give good gifts than human parents do (see Matt. 7:9-11). He said the Father is more disposed to supply need than a friend is (see Luke 11:5-13). He also said that God is

" 'Ask, and it shall be given to you; seek, and you shall find; knock, and it shall be opened to you. For everyone who asks receives, and he who seeks finds, and to him who knocks it shall be opened' " (Matt. 7:7-8).

36

more ready to dispense justice than an earthly judge is (see Luke 18:1-8). In each of these illustrations Jesus pictured God as going far beyond any human measure. If an earthly father will give good gifts to his child, how much more will the Heavenly Father do so (see Matt. 7:11)? If an unjust judge will administer protection, will God delay long in providing for His elect (see Luke 18:7)?

What will God give? The contexts of Jesus' invitations to ask are all found in sections on the kingdom, which is our highest interest. To bring the kingdom, God will give: " 'what you need' " (Matt. 6:8); " 'good gifts' " and " 'what is good' " (Matt. 7:11); " 'anything that [two agreed] they may ask' " (Matt. 18:19); " 'all things you ask in prayer, believing' " (Matt. 21:22); " 'whatever you ask in My name' " (John 14:13); and, most comprehensive of all, " 'anything' " (John 16:23). Jesus set no limits on what God is willing to give, and He described it all as good. Of course, Jesus' own prayer life and priorities illustrate the necessity of asking in God's will (see Matt. 6:10; 26:39,42; John 5:30; 6:38; 17:4).

Jesus set no limits on what God is willing to give, and He described it all as good.

Match each of the six petitions in the Model Prayer (Matt. 6:9-13) with the correct summary description.

___ 1. **"Our Father who art in heaven, Hallowed be Thy name."**

___ 2. **"Thy kingdom come."**

___ 3. **"Thy will be done, On earth as it is in heaven."**

___ 4. **"Give us this day our daily bread."**

___ 5. **"And forgive us our debts, as we also have forgiven our debtors."**

___ 6. **"And do not lead us into temptation, but deliver us from evil."**

a. **For the accomplishment of His purposes on earth**

b. **For forgiveness**

c. **For protection from temptation**

d. **For His sovereignty**

e. **For the holiness of God's name**

f. **For physical needs**

Jesus Taught the Importance of Prayer

Jesus repeatedly taught the importance of prayer in a believer's life.

Persistence. Two of Jesus' most powerful parables encouraged His disciples to pray persistently. In Luke 11:5-13 He pictured one who should have been favorably disposed, a friend, who yielded to an insistent demand for an emergency food supply. In Luke 18:1-8 He told of one unfavorably disposed, an unjust judge, who yielded to a widow's stubborn suit for protection. In both parables Jesus centered on the character of the supplicant rather than the one addressed and presented persistence as a character trait that is pleasing to God. In the first parable Jesus concluded, " 'Even though he will not get up and give him anything because he is his friend, yet because of his persistence he will get up and give him as much as he needs' " (Luke 11:8). Persistence secured as much as or more than the original request for three loaves. Clearly, God is even more willing than a friend to respond to our needs (see vv. 9-10).

In the second parable the same idea of God's willingness to go beyond our expectations is evident. After demonstrating the judge's willingness to yield to persistence, Jesus gave one of the most thrilling pictures in Scripture of God's readiness to hear: " 'Hear what the unrighteous judge said; now shall not God bring about justice for His elect, who cry to Him day and night, and will He delay long over them? I tell you that He will bring about justice for them speedily' " (Luke 18:6-8). This parable is a study in contrasts. God is not at all like the unrighteous judge. He is eager to hear the cries of His people.

It may seem strange that God should require importunity, or insistence. Biblical examples of importunity furnish us with many object lessons about its value. Persistence gives us time to be sure of what we want and of what God prefers to give in His desire for our good. In Abraham's reiterated requests to spare Sodom and Gomorrah, he began with a dwarfed conception of God, fearing that God would destroy a community of 50 righteous who were pocketed in sinful cities. He ended with a magnificent understanding of God's holiness and mercy; God would have spared Sodom even if there had been only 10 righteous in the city (see Gen. 18:20-32). God allowed Abraham to continue because although Abraham, in his ignorance of the number of righteous in Sodom, could not have known the impossibility of his petition, it would have been in God's character to spare Sodom if there *had* been 50 righteous. This tells us that it is all right to persist in prayer if the character of the petition is within the character of God.

Persistence gives us time to be sure of what we want and of what God prefers to give in His desire for our good.

Importunity proves and establishes earnestness. The word for *importunity* can mean *shamelessness*. The earnestness of the Capernaum nobleman obtained through persistence what he asked (see John 4:46-54). Peter's release from prison followed a prayer by the church that was made for him "fervently" (Acts 12:5), which literally means "stretched-outedly."

Promises. The promises Jesus gave about prayer are limitless. His emphasis was on the human activity—ask and receive, seek and find, knock and watch the door open. The implication is that God reacts favorably to the earnestness of His people. There can be no limitation on the divine ability to perform or the divine goodwill to give. If there is a limitation, it is on the human imagination or faith. The imagination may be limited by a small conception of God's nature and resources, by a lack of understanding about God's goodness, or by any number of spiritual disabilities. Faith may be limited by inadequate knowledge of God's Word, by spiritual blindness, and sometimes by inexperience. Much we experience in daily living tends to dull spiritual imagination and faith. Jesus challenged us out of the quagmire of unbelief by giving promises that cannot be bound by human conception: we may ask "whatever" or "anything" (John 14:13-14).

Unified prayer. Jesus attached a special condition and a special significance to one of His promises. If two or three are gathered in His name, He is in their midst, and the Father will do anything they agree to ask. My wife and I discovered the enormous potential of truly unified prayer during the dark days of her chemotherapy for cancer. As God united our spirits with His through the agonizing search to discover His purposes, we found our own spirits knit together in the tightest agreement we had ever known—agreement with His intentions, identity with His holiness, and mutuality in our life purposes. Although we had always practiced family devotions, the joy in our mutual prayer dramatically increased. And so did the dimensions of our prayer life together! As the bond grew tighter, our faith increased, and our prayers were answered in dimensions we had never known. We prayed when my wife developed shingles; all symptoms disappeared in three days. On another occasion we prayed for a computer. Without any knowledge of our need or our prayer, a businessman in our city provided the funds for a computer. We discovered a principle: bonding in faith increases faith; the closer the bond, the more powerful the prayer.

*What a friend we have
  in Jesus,
All our sins and griefs
  to bear!
What a privilege to carry
Everything to God
  in prayer!*[4]
—*Joseph Scriven (1819–66),
Irish immigrant to Canada
who performed menial work
and suffered much hardship*

◖◦✿◦◗

Read Matthew 18:19-20 from at least two translations.

In your own words summarize these verses in no more than two sentences.

_____

_____

What is the value or advantage of praying with others?

_____

_____

The Holy Spirit, Our Helper in Prayer

One exciting aspect of learning a language is discovering that certain ideas are peculiar to a given language and cannot be adequately translated into another. English speakers need much experience to distinguish between *conocer* and *saber* (*to know*) in Spanish, but a native speaker easily uses the two verbs correctly and would never confuse the two different concepts. As I was learning Japanese years ago, I was thrilled to discover that certain ideas important in the Japanese mentality are not thinkable in English. In Japanese I could think thoughts I had never thought before!

The same limitation applies to the different areas of human experience within the confines of any given language. I could describe musical phenomena in scientific language, but if I limit my description to the vocabulary of science alone, I will leave out some of the most important aspects of what music really is. A color-blind person might understand the mechanism of the light spectrum and perhaps even the structuring of cone cells in the eye that receive the various levels of the spectrum, but anyone else knows red and green in a way that the color-blind person cannot.

Paul tells us that human beings have this same difficulty thinking in spiritual terms: "A natural man does not accept the things

40

of the Spirit of God; for they are foolishness to him, and he cannot understand them, because they are spiritually appraised" (1 Cor. 2:14). For this reason all our attempts to explain a mystery as great as the Trinity are frustrated by language itself. For example, when we describe the functions of the Persons of the Trinity, we sometimes do an injustice to our understanding of the unity of the Godhead.

Scripture does not assume that it is necessary to understand these mysteries. It is more important to know God than to understand God. God was revealed in the Old Testament basically as one, but implicit through that revelation were indications of His plurality. Jesus did not repeal the faith of Israel that God is one but emphasized it (see Mark 12:29-30). The New Testament assumes throughout that God is one. Yet it also presents the functions of the three Persons of the Trinity. The New Testament writers saw no conflict in this emphasis on the three Persons of the Trinity and the unity of God as one.

Thus, the third Person of the Trinity may properly be called the Holy Spirit, the "Spirit of Jesus Christ" (Phil. 1:19), or the " 'Spirit of the Lord' " (Acts 5:9). He is the "Spirit of Christ" (Rom. 8:9), and yet Christ sent Him from the Father (see John 15:26), just as Christ identified Himself with the Father (see John 10:30; 14:9-11), and yet the Father sent Christ (see John 6:38). The Holy Spirit performs as Jesus performed, thinks as Jesus thinks, pleads as Jesus pleads. His present work is an exact continuation of Christ's work.

It is more important to know God than to understand God.

Answer the true/false statements by writing a *T* or an *F* in the blank beside each statement.

___ 1. Little is said in the New Testament about the Holy Spirit.

___ 2. Christ's work in the world stopped with His ascension to heaven.

___ 3. The Holy Spirit dwells only in believers' lives.

___ 4. The Holy Spirit does not dwell in every believer.

___ 5. The Holy Spirit helps us pray.

___ 6. Our prayers should deal with generalities, not with specifics.

___ 7. To truly know God's will, a person must be willing to obey and follow God's will.

"Do you not know that your body is a temple of the Holy Spirit who is in you, whom you have from God, and that you are not your own?"
(1 Cor. 6:19).

Check your responses as you explore the Holy Spirit's role in your prayer life.

The Holy Spirit Is the Indwelling Presence of Christ

The indwelling presence of Christ is the Spirit that Jesus promised the disciples. He told them that the Spirit would indwell them: " 'I will ask the Father, and He will give you another Helper, that He may be with you forever; that is the Spirit of truth, whom the world cannot receive, because it does not behold Him or know Him, but you know Him because He abides with you, and will be in you' " (John 14:16-17). Because the Holy Spirit dwells in the believer, the very body of the believer is the temple of the Holy Spirit (see 1 Cor. 6:19).

Yet after stating that the Spirit is " 'another Helper,' " Christ immediately identified Himself with the Spirit: " 'I will not leave you as orphans; I will come to you' " (John 14:18). The Holy Spirit is the indwelling presence of Christ for every believer.

This indwelling Spirit also sanctifies (see 1 Pet. 1:2), and that too is the will and work of Christ (see John 17:19; 1 Cor. 1:30). God expressed His love in sending the Son (see 1 John 4:10); God poured out His love through the Holy Spirit in the hearts of those justified by faith (see Rom. 5:5). The work of Christ and the work of the Holy Spirit are pure expressions of all God is and of all He intends for His people.

The Holy Spirit is indispensable to a Christian's prayer life. We have access to the Father through Christ (see Eph. 2:18). Access to any throne is only through the strictest protocol; admission to the throne of the universe is available only through Christ. Our access to the Father is through Christ and is made real by the Spirit who lives within us. Spiritual prayer—prayer that is effective—is prayer led by the Holy Spirit.

The Holy Spirit Continues the Work of Christ

The Holy Spirit makes Christ's teachings and purposes, including prayer, real to the believer. The disciples knew that Christ's purposes for them must be accomplished in their lives. They had learned much from Christ, but there was much yet to learn. Jesus told them, " 'I have many more things to say to you, but you cannot bear them now' " (John 16:12). He had assured them only moments before, " 'The Helper, the Holy Spirit, whom the Father will send in My name, He will teach you all things, and bring to your remembrance all that I said to you' " (John 14:26). Christ's departure need not threaten the loss of what they had learned; the Holy Spirit would restore it to memory and would bring new understandings that would harmonize with those of Christ. The revelation would be completed: " 'When He, the Spirit of truth, comes, He will guide you into all the truth' " (John 16:13). Just as Christ did not work independently, on His own initiative (see John 5:30), the Spirit " 'will not speak on His own initiative, but whatever He hears, He will speak; and He will disclose to you what is to come' " (John 16:13). Christ revealed the Father's nature and will; the Holy Spirit continues to reveal Christ's teachings and purposes.

The Holy Spirit continues to reveal Christ's teachings and purposes.

One of Christ's temptations had been to submit to Satan, the prince of this world, in order to have " 'the kingdoms of the world, and their glory' " (Matt. 4:8). Jesus later cautioned the disciples, " 'I am not of this world' " (John 8:23) and stated in His High-Priestly prayer that the disciples themselves were given Him " 'out of the world' " (John 17:6). Twice later in the same prayer He declared that they were " 'not of the world' " (vv. 14,16). Paul wrote, "We have received, not the spirit of the world, but the Spirit who is from God, that we might know the things freely given to us by God, which things we also speak, not in words taught by human wisdom, but in those taught by the Spirit, combining spiritual thoughts with spiritual words" (1 Cor. 2:12-13). Whatever the Spirit taught them, it would not contradict what they had learned but would continue in the same vein as what Christ had taught. It would be in the Spirit of Christ, and it would fulfill all Christ started.

The Holy Spirit Helps Us Know God's Will

Jesus had taught the disciples to pray, " 'Thy will be done' " (Matt. 6:10). Evidently, they did not fully understand how serious this plea should be, for later James; John; and their mother, Salome, approached Jesus with a request that was unanswerable at that time. They asked that they, James and John, sit on the Lord's right hand in His kingdom. The error in their request was one that has caused difficulty for Christians throughout history. Their petition involved things they could not understand. Jesus explained, " 'You do not know what you are asking for.' " They wanted positions of honor, but Jesus asked, in turn, another question that revealed a necessary consequence of such honor: " 'Are you able to drink the cup that I am about to drink?' " (Matt. 20:22). Jesus wanted them to understand the implications of their request. This request angered the other disciples and demonstrated an ignorance of true greatness in the kingdom, as Jesus pointed out in verses 26-28.

It is encouraging to see that this kind of mistake early in life need not persist, for it was this same John who could write with joyous assurance, after much experience and many years, "This is the confidence which we have before Him, that, if we ask anything according to His will, He hears us" (1 John 5:14). In the course of his life after the incident recorded in Matthew 20, John had learned to pray, " 'Thy will be done' " (Matt. 6:10), just as He had been taught, and later, he recorded the assurance that God will answer prayer that is made in His will.

God's will was one of Jesus' major concerns. As a boy He "had to be in the things of His Father" (a more literal translation of Luke 2:49). Early in His career, before the start of His Galilean ministry, He told some of His disciples, " 'My food is to do the will of Him who sent Me, and to accomplish His work' " (John 4:34). Later, in a controversy over the Sabbath He claimed, " 'My judgment is just, because I do not seek My own will, but the will of Him who sent Me' " (John 5:30). Some time after that, He told a group in Capernaum, " 'I have come down from heaven, not to do My own will, but the will of Him who sent Me' " (John 6:38). Finally, at the end of His life He could claim that He had accomplished the work the Father had given Him to do (see John 17:4). Even in Gethsemane Jesus accepted the cup because it was His Father's will (see Matt. 26:39,42). God's will was of such importance to Him that the author of Hebrews 10:7 saw in Psalm 40:7-8 a messianic utterance:

> *Then I said, "Behold, I come;*
> *In the scroll of the book it is written of me;*
> *I delight to do Thy will, O my God;*
> *Thy Law is within my heart."*

Significantly, Jesus' devotion to God's will became a major concern of His followers. John's confidence in prayers made according to God's will (see 1 John 5:14) is also emphasized in 1 John 3:22. Jesus' half-brother James learned to govern his conversation by God's will (see Jas. 4:15). God's will was of major importance to

God's will was one of Jesus' major concerns.

Peter. He stated that doing right, in God's will, would silence the ignorance of foolish men (see 1 Pet. 2:15). Those who suffer according to God's will should entrust their souls to God's faithfulness to do what is right (see 1 Pet. 4:19), and pastors should function voluntarily, according to God's will (see 1 Pet. 5:2). Also running throughout Paul's writings is a recurrent theme of seeking and performing God's will. Paul's actions were dependent on God's will (see Acts 13:2; 16:6; 20:23; Rom. 1:10). Paul even persuaded others to accept God's will (see Acts 21:14).

The Holy Spirit helps us understand God's will. The church in Antioch knew God's will through the Holy Spirit: "While they were ministering to the Lord and fasting, the Holy Spirit said, 'Set apart for Me Barnabas and Saul for the work to which I have called them' " (Acts 13:2). Note that the Holy Spirit had already called Barnabas and Saul. The Holy Spirit forbade Paul to go into Asia (see Acts 16:6)—a prohibition that rerouted the gospel into Europe. As Paul said good-bye to the church in Ephesus, he stated that the Holy Spirit had testified to him about the bonds and afflictions awaiting him (see Acts 20:23). Paul wrote that the things of God can be known only through the Spirit of God: "To us God revealed them [the things God has prepared for those who love Him] through the Spirit; for the Spirit searches all things, even the depths of God. For who among men knows the thoughts of a man except the spirit of the man, which is in him? Even so the thoughts of God no one knows except the Spirit of God" (1 Cor. 2:10-11).

How can we know God's will? The Bible, inspired by the Holy Spirit, is one source of revelation: "All Scripture is inspired by God and profitable for teaching, for reproof, for correction, for training in righteousness; that the man of God may be adequate, equipped for every good work" (2 Tim. 3:16-17). The psalmist declared that the testimony of the Lord makes wise the simple and the commandment of the Lord enlightens the eyes (see Ps. 19:7-8). The Bible reveals the kind of thoughts God thinks, as they concern us, and the patterns those thoughts follow.

We can also know God's will through prayer. Paul assured the Colossian church, "We have not ceased to pray for you and to ask that you may be filled with the knowledge of His will in all spiritual wisdom and understanding" (Col. 1:9). Jesus' prayer life is the most convincing proof in the Bible of the Holy Spirit's work in revealing God's will. "Full of the Holy Spirit" (Luke 4:1), Jesus was

"Teach me to do Thy will, For Thou art my God; Let Thy good Spirit lead me on level ground" (Ps. 143:10).

45

"led up by the Spirit" to His temptation (see Matt. 4:1). After the temptation He returned to Galilee "in the power of the Spirit" (Luke 4:14). He " 'cast out demons by the Spirit of God' " (see Matt. 12:28). Jesus' earthly life was totally controlled by the Spirit of God because He prayed habitually. He prayed in times of decision, as when He chose the twelve, and He prayed in times of crisis, as in Gethsemane.

We cannot pray for the Spirit's direction unless we are willing to do God's will.

We cannot pray for the Spirit's direction unless we are willing to do God's will. Jesus repeatedly emphasized the importance of the human will and of openness to hear from God. He asked the Pharisees, " 'Why do you not understand what I am saying? It is because you cannot hear My word' " (John 8:43). Unwillingness to accept God's revelation blinded them. Unwillingness is deliberate. Jesus, quoting from Isaiah 6:10, said that the Jews had " 'closed their eyes' " (Matt. 13:15).

Later Jesus declared, " 'He who is of God hears the words of God' " (John 8:47). Hearing is a live option; Jesus often invited, " 'He who has ears to hear, let him hear' " (Mark 4:9). Jesus used the tender figure of a shepherd and sheep to describe how naturally His sheep should hear His voice: " 'To him [the shepherd] the doorkeeper opens, and the sheep hear his voice, and he calls his own sheep by name, and leads them out. When he puts forth all his own, he goes before them, and the sheep follow him because they know his voice. And a stranger they simply will not follow, but will flee from him, because they do not know the voice of strangers' " (John 10:3-5). He told the disciples, " 'Blessed are your eyes, because they see; and your ears, because they hear' " (Matt. 13:16).

God is willing to give wisdom liberally; all we have to do is ask (see Jas. 1:5). Asking involves a willing spirit. A willing spirit enables us to recognize divine teaching: " 'If any man is willing to do His [God's] will, he shall know of the teaching, whether it is of God, or whether I speak from Myself' " (John 7:17). To hear from the Holy Spirit what God's will is, it is absolutely essential that we come to prayer desiring God's will, asking for God's will, and being disposed to carry out God's will if it involves action.

⊱⚜⊰

Suppose that a new believer asks you the following questions about the Holy Spirit. Write your responses in the boxes on page 47.

Who is the Holy Spirit?

How do you know that the Holy Spirit lives in you?

How does the Holy Spirit help you pray?

How does the Holy Spirit help you know God's will for your life?

Trust and obey, for there's no other way
To be happy in Jesus, but to trust and obey.[5]
—John H. Sammis (1846–1919), Presbyterian pastor and teacher

What difference does the Holy Spirit make in your life?

47

The Holy Spirit Is Our Guide and Helper

The Holy Spirit is the believer's guide and helper in prayer. People have sensed a need for guidance and help in discerning God's will throughout history. Long ago Jeremiah pleaded with God,

> *I know, O Lord, that a man's way is not in himself;*
> *Nor is it in a man who walks to direct his steps.*
> *Correct me, O Lord, but with justice;*
> *Not with Thine anger, lest Thou bring me to nothing (Jer. 10:23-24).*

"The best prayers have often more groans than words."[6]
—*John Bunyan (1628–88), English preacher and author of* The Pilgrim's Progress, *who was imprisoned for his fearless preaching*

With the advent of the Christian message and the indwelling of the Spirit of God, Jeremiah's ancient plea found its answer, an answer available to every believer: "In the same way the Spirit also helps our weakness; for we do not know how to pray as we should, but the Spirit Himself intercedes for us with groanings too deep for words; and He who searches the hearts knows what the mind of the Spirit is, because He intercedes for the saints according to the will of God" (Rom. 8:26-27).

In verse 26 the word *help* is the same word Martha used in Luke 10:40 when she asked Jesus to require Mary's help in the kitchen. The help of the Holy Spirit is useful for accomplishing specific tasks. The specific weakness He helps in this case is our inadequate knowledge of how to pray. He helps with unutterable groanings, with depth of meaning to the divine mind far beyond where human language can venture. The intercession is for—on behalf of—the saints and is always in perfect accordance with God's will. The Spirit translates our awkward prayers into the noble and high intentions of God Himself, who gives only good and perfect gifts (see Jas. 1:17).

Read Romans 8:26-27 from at least two translations. Then write what you believe Paul meant when he said that the Spirit "intercedes for us with groanings too deep for words."

_____

_____

The name of the Holy Spirit in the Lord's final discourse is often translated Helper (see John 14:26; 15:26; 16:7). Here the word *Helper* means *one called alongside, that is, to help.*

The Holy Spirit serves as our guide into all truth (see John 16:13). His very name is " 'Spirit of truth' " (John 15:26; 16:13), and He leads us into all truth. There is no limit to how much of the Spirit's help we can have. John the Baptist assured us that Christ gives the Spirit without measure (see John 3:34).

There is no limit to how much of the Spirit's help we can have.

Because the Holy Spirit knows God's will and is our guide and helper in prayer, it is important that our minds, lives, hearts, purposes, and activities be filled with Him. If someone says, "That speaker is full of his subject," most of us understand what he means. If I say that a boy is "full of football," most people understand that football permeates his thinking and talk in school, at the table, at play, and in church. He has placed football ahead of everything else, and football dominates all he does. Believers are commended to be continually filled with the Spirit (see Eph. 5:18). Our orientation to everything in life is to be spiritual. If we are filled with the Spirit, His mind and purpose take precedence over every attitude. The Spirit governs our thinking, is the major influence in every decision, and is observable in all our actions.

We are to pray in the Spirit. This is not possible unless we are filled with the Spirit: "With all prayer and petition pray at all times in the Spirit" (Eph. 6:18). The key word is *all*. Every petition, every prayer proceeds from the mind of the Spirit, not from selfish motives or self-serving ends. Jude made this same lesson graphic by first giving the opposite of spiritual praying (often we can understand a concept by thinking of its opposite): "These are the ones who cause divisions, worldly-minded, devoid of the Spirit" (Jude 19). Jude then piled up phrases describing the accompaniment of praying in the Spirit: "But you, beloved, building yourselves up on your most holy faith; praying in the Holy Spirit; keep yourselves in the love of God, waiting anxiously for the mercy of our Lord Jesus Christ to eternal life" (Jude 20-21).

Praying in the Spirit does not rule out praying with the mind. The mind provides our prayers with precise meaning. Praying in generalities obtains answers in general. It is not enough to pray, "Be with us," for God is always with us. We need to ask for the specific purpose of God's presence in our lives.

Teach me to pray, Lord,
teach me to pray;
This is my heart-cry
day unto day;
I long to know thy will
and Thy way;
Teach me to pray, Lord,
teach me to pray.

Power in prayer, Lord,
power in prayer!
Here 'mid earth's sin
and sorrow and care,
Men lost and dying,
souls in despair;
O give me power,
power in prayer!

Teach me to pray, Lord,
teach me to pray;
Thou art my pattern
day unto day;
Thou art my surety,
now and for aye;
Teach me to pray, Lord,
teach me to pray.

Living in Thee, Lord,
and Thou in me,
Constantly abiding,
this is my plea;
Grant me Thy power,
boundless and free,
Power with men
and power with Thee.[7]

The mind is an instrument for ordering our prayers. The psalmist spoke of laying his requests before God daily (see Ps. 5:3). Still God's power is unleashed through the Spirit. The word of the Lord to Zerubbabel was " 'Not by might nor by power, but by My Spirit' " (Zech. 4:6). We need not fear mindless abandon if God's Spirit is in control. Praying that pleases God is in neither mindless spirit nor spiritless mind. Rather, it is prayer in which the mind is tuned to the frequency of the Holy Spirit, who is in control.

The Holy Spirit is available to us, is in us, and is alongside us. He glorifies Christ, enlightens our minds, opens God's will to us, guides us, and helps our prayers, both as we utter them on earth and as they are interpreted in heaven. We cannot accomplish Christ's work without the prayer-help of the Holy Spirit.

[1]Marcus Rainsford, *Our Lord Prays for His Own: Thoughts on John 17* (Chicago: Moody Press, 1950), 40.

[2]M. E. Dodd, *The Prayer Life of Jesus* (Nashville: The Sunday School Board of the Southern Baptist Convention, 1923), 16.

[3]George Newton, *An Exposition of John 17* (Carlisle, PA: The Banner of Truth Trust, 1995), 390.

[4]Joseph Scriven, "What a Friend We Have in Jesus," in *The Baptist Hymnal* (Nashville: Convention Press, 1991), 182.

[5]John H. Sammis, "Trust and Obey," in *The Baptist Hymnal,* 447.

[6]John Bunyan, in *The One-Year Book of Personal Prayer* (Wheaton, IL: Tyndale House, 1991), September 8.

[7]Albert S. Reitz, "Teach Me to Pray." © copyright 1925 renewal 1953 Broadman Press. All rights reserved. International copyright secured. Used by permission.

Answers to activities:
Pages 30–31: 1. T, 2. F, 3. T, 4. F, 5. T, 6. F, 7. F, 8. T
Page 37: 1. e, 2. d, 3. a, 4. f, 5. b, 6. c
Page 41: 1. F, 2. F, 3. T, 4. F, 5. T, 6. F, 7. T

Chapter 3
Prayer That Transforms

Prayer is fellowship with God (see 1 John 1:3) and grows from a relationship with God so multifaceted that no single form of prayer exhausts all the potential of that relationship. The Bible provides us with multiple pictures of our relationship with God. Sometimes our relationship is that of a Father and child; sometimes of a Master and servant; at other times of an older Brother and other family members, of a Teacher and disciple, and of a Leader and follower. This is one reason the Old Testament gives us so many names for God (the Almighty, the Holy One, Rock, Refuge) and the New Testament supplies additional names for Christ (Bread, Door, Shepherd, Friend, High Priest). In the same way that we cannot exhaust all that God is with human words, we cannot limit our dialogue with Him to one kind of prayer.

There are many kinds of prayer because there are many aspects of our relationship with God. At times His greatness is the primary focus, such as when that which is created praises the Creator. At times His beneficence is primary, when we speak gratefully to our Benefactor. In time of need we are supplicant, and God is Source. The various aspects of His limitless nature alternately move in and out of our vision as we need His mercy, His provision, His protection, His strength, or simply His smile. People pray in many different ways for many different reasons. The Model Prayer (Matt. 6:9-15), often referred to as the Lord's Prayer, provides us with an outline that covers most of the major directions prayer takes.

"What we have seen and heard we proclaim to you also, that you also may have fellowship with us; and indeed our fellowship is with the Father, and with His Son Jesus Christ" (1 John 1:3).

Prayers of Adoration

The Model Prayer begins in worship—with a recognition of God's nature and identity. He is, above all and first of all, Father, and He is spiritual—" 'who art in heaven' " (Matt. 6:9). The fact that He is in heaven does not mean that He is distant from us on earth but that He is different from the world; the God we pray to is spiritual.

Jesus said we are to worship God in spirit and in truth (see John

4:24). This difficult concept may best be understood by comparing it to its opposite. The opposite of worship in spirit is anything that limits God to time or space as our physical senses perceive it.

There is no correct hour of prayer, although it is helpful to order our day so that, for example, we begin the day with prayer. There is also no fixed place to which prayer is limited, although certain places are important to the believer in praying—a place alone, the family devotions, or the assembling of believers. What is the opposite of worship in truth? The opposite is praying in meaningless formula, in insincerity, in falsity of doctrine or attitude.

Worshiping God for His attributes. We are to hallow, or recognize as holy, God's name, or identity. But this is only a beginning. The Model Prayer is suggestive, not exhaustive. The Bible is full of other kinds of adoration. We worship God for all of His attributes, and the Bible always gives precedence to holiness. Again and again in the great encounters with God, great people of God first saw His holiness—Moses (see Ex. 3:5), Isaiah (see Isa. 6:3), and Peter (see Luke 5:8). Recognition of His holiness formed an introductory part of the profound prayers of Hannah (see 1 Sam. 2:2) and Mary (see Luke 1:49).

Biblical praise also manifests many other attributes of God. The psalmist praised Him for His majesty and greatness (see Ps. 104:1; also see Isa. 9:6), His splendor and strength (see Ps. 96:6), His character (see Ps. 18:2-3), His glory (see Ps. 19:1), and the joy of His presence (see Ps. 84). Many psalms are songs of pure praise (see Pss. 103; 106; 111—113; 117; 135; 146—148). Some are hymns to His majesty (see Pss. 8; 19; 24; 29; 48; 50; 76; 93; 97), and some are joyful expressions of abandon (see Pss. 47; 66; 81; 148).

Study Psalm 103 from two translations. Record the benefits or blessings for which David praised God.

> *"Let prayers be the key of the morning, and the bolt of the evening."*
> —Matthew Henry (1662–1714), English pastor and Scripture commentator

52

_____ _____ _____

_____ _____ _____

_____ _____ _____

_____ _____ _____

_____ _____ _____

Now read aloud the list you have made, personalizing the benefits as you read. For example, "He has forgiven me of my sins."

Circle five benefits you listed that are most important to you. Spend time praising God for all of His benefits.

We have many other reasons to adore and praise God in prayer. *God is infinite.* God's qualities are not measurable by any standard we know. We cannot understand infinity, but we can stand in awe of God, who is infinite.

- The psalmist marveled, "He telleth the number of the stars; he calleth them all by their names. Great is our Lord, and of great power: his understanding is infinite" (Ps. 147:4-5, KJV).
- Isaiah wondered, "Hast thou not known? Hast thou not heard, that the everlasting God, the Lord, the Creator of the ends of the earth, fainteth not, neither is weary? There is no searching of his understanding" (Isa. 40:28, KJV).
- This attitude of wonder and awe is maintained throughout the psalms; contemplating how God reverses the ways of men, the psalmist exclaimed, "This is the Lord's doing [this placing of the stone which the builders rejected as the chief cornerstone]; it is marvelous in our eyes" (Ps. 118:23, KJV).

God is transcendent. We are also to stand in awe of God because He is above and beyond anything else we know; He is other than any of His creatures. Theologians call this quality of otherness *transcendence.* The psalmist expressed it in awesome words: "Who is like unto the Lord our God, who dwelleth on high?" (Ps. 113:5, KJV). He is so vastly beyond anything we can know that Solomon asked, "Will God indeed dwell on the earth? Behold, the heaven

"Our praise and worship should be like this: 'Lord, sinner as I am, weak as I am , fallen as I am, thank You for the grace that reached down and lifted me up and set me a saint, a called-out one, separated one into Your kingdom! Thank You, Lord, for remembering me. Thank You, God, for saving me. Thank You, Lord, for being good to me.' "[2]
—*W. A. Criswell (1909– 2002), pastor of First Baptist Church; Dallas, Texas*

and heaven of heavens cannot contain thee; how much less this house that I have builded?" (1 Kings 8:27, KJV).

God is unique. We attribute worth to God because of His uniqueness. Hannah acknowledged, "There is none holy as the Lord: for there is none beside thee: neither is there any rock like our God" (1 Sam. 2:2, KJV). Paul told us that "there is no power but of God: the powers that be are ordained of God" (Rom. 13:1, KJV). God's uniqueness prompted the command "Thou shalt worship no other god: for the Lord, whose name is Jealous, is a jealous God" (Ex. 34:14, KJV). God is the source of all holiness, all strength, all authority. His worth stands alone; nothing is on a par with Him.

God is wise. We can attribute worth to God because of His wisdom and knowledge. Paul, who often broke into a doxology as he contemplated God's glory, said, "O the depth of the riches both of the wisdom and knowledge of God! How unsearchable are his judgments, and his ways past finding out!" (Rom. 11:33, KJV).

God is completely perfect. God's worth is seen in the completeness, the totality, of each of His perfections. The psalmist said, "The judgments of the Lord are true and righteous altogether" (Ps. 19:9, KJV) and "The Lord is righteous in all his ways, and holy in all his works" (Ps. 145:17, KJV). This totality of His perfection separates Him from His creatures. We must acknowledge His worth in "worth-ship." He is worthy to be praised![3]

In the New Testament Paul sometimes concluded his arguments with a doxology: "Oh, the depth of the riches both of the wisdom and knowledge of God! How unsearchable are His judgments and unfathomable His ways! ... For from Him and through Him and to Him are all things. To Him be the glory forever. Amen" (Rom. 11:33-36).

Worshiping God for His creative power. Many biblical expressions of praise treat at length God's creative power. The main theme of Psalm 104 is expressed in verse 24. Read that verse in the margin.

The rest of the psalm rapturously describes the Lord moving through His possessions (see vv. 2-4), creating them (see vv. 5-9), and maintaining them (see vv. 10-32). Creation is also a major theme in many other psalms (see Pss. 8; 19; 24; 50; 66; 93; 97—98). The praise for creation and in creation assumes cosmic proportions in the last three psalms of the psalter (see Pss. 148—150).

Worshiping God for His role in history. Another important form

"O Lord, how many are Thy works! In wisdom Thou hast made them all; The earth is full of Thy possessions" (Ps. 104:24).

54

of praise in the Old Testament is a recounting of history with a view to God's role in it. Exodus 15 is a tribute to God's supernatural actions in delivering Israel out of Egypt. Several psalms tell of Israel's history as God acted on its behalf (Pss. 78; 105—106; 114; 135—136). These are important because Israel so quickly forgot what God did for the nation. Perhaps if it had remembered, it would not have complained in the desert or would not have gone after false gods.

Worshiping God for His work in Christ. These Old Testament praise-histories prepared the way for a similar type of praise in the New Testament as believers praised God for what He had done for them in Christ. Peter extolled God as a Father who acted: "Blessed be the God and Father of our Lord Jesus Christ, who according to His great mercy has caused us to be born again to a living hope through the resurrection of Jesus Christ from the dead, to obtain an inheritance which is imperishable and undefiled and will not fade away, reserved in heaven for you" (1 Pet. 1:3-4). Paul also exclaimed, "Blessed be the God and Father of our Lord Jesus Christ, who has blessed us with every spiritual blessing in the heavenly places in Christ" (Eph. 1:3) and continued with a three-fold doxology that indicated the praiseworthiness of the grace of each Person of the Trinity (of the Father in Eph. 1:6, of the Son in Eph. 1:12, and of the Holy Spirit in Eph. 1:13-14).

New Testament believers praised God for what He had done for them in Christ.

At one time I was experiencing personal and private grief. Without realizing it, I stopped praising God as I prayed. Although I begged God for relief from the grief, no relief came. I struggled through five praiseless days in this dark mood. Finally, I realized that if I praised God on the mountaintop but refused to praise Him in the valley, I was not praising God at all—I was praising my feelings. I did not feel like praising, but I also knew that much of our commitment to God is a matter of the will, not of feelings. God had not changed! His glory, His majesty, and His eternal purpose were not dimmed or tainted by the events of my life. So I went to my prayer closet, kneeled before the Lord, and concentrated on His unchanging perfections.

I knew that I was still much blessed. My salvation was intact; my family was godly; my job was secure. The dark days had made me concentrate on the unhappiness of the hurt. So I sang the Doxology to the Lord—"praise God from whom all blessings flow!" I began to feel a lightness in my spirit that I had not sensed for days. Then I quoted to the Lord Psalm 103 with its staggering list of benefits. By now the lightness was becoming joy in the Lord's presence, and I marveled at the inner change that praise had worked so quickly.[4]

Jesus began the Model Prayer by acknowledging God's position and nature. This beginning places things in perspective. This perspective is basic to true prayer. Worship is the human appreciation of and adoration of God, and it places all we pray in proper relationship and perspective.

Thanking God for His goodness. Closely related to praise in the Bible is thanksgiving. Praise and thanksgiving are often mentioned together in the psalms:

Praise the Lord!
Oh give thanks to the Lord, for He is good;
For His lovingkindness is everlasting (Ps. 106:1).

The psalmist said that praise and thanksgiving declare God's character:

It is good to give thanks to the Lord,
And to sing praises to Thy name, O Most High;
To declare Thy lovingkindness in the morning,
And Thy faithfulness by night (Ps. 92:1-2).

Through Moses, God gave a commandment that when the offering of firstfruits was brought to the Lord, the Jewish citizen was to pray, " 'Now behold, I have brought the first of the produce of the ground which Thou, O Lord hast given me.' " The commandment continues: " 'You shall set it down before the Lord your God, and worship before the Lord your God; and you and the Levite and the alien who is among you shall rejoice in all the good which the Lord your God has given you and your household' " (Deut. 26:10-11).

Squeezing toothpaste onto my toothbrush one morning, I realized that I had never thanked God for toothpaste. Come to think of it, I had never thanked Him for my teeth. I wondered: *What if my blessings tomorrow depended on my thanksgiving today? It would mean that if I did not thank God for air and lungs today, there would be no air tomorrow, and my lungs would collapse!*

Few of us realize our total dependence on God. We fail to acknowledge God as the source of everything we have. He is our source for abundant living, bestowing on us material and spiritual blessings according to His grace.[5]

This is what thanksgiving is about—it declares our understanding of what is good. We rejoice in it and acknowledge its source. Thanksgiving is rejoicing in what God declares to be good and is important because it establishes our relationship to our Source.

The word *all* becomes important when the Bible talks about thanksgiving. Many people assume that we thank God only for what we perceive to be blessings. Such an attitude obviously grows from and leads to materialism. Paul wrote, "In everything give thanks; for this is God's will for you in Christ Jesus" (1 Thess. 5:18). We can give thanks in all things, for all things, only if we are convinced that "God causes all things to work together for good to those who love God, to those who are called according to His purpose" (Rom. 8:28).

The attitude of thanksgiving is also to permeate our petitions: "Be anxious for nothing, but in everything by prayer and supplication with thanksgiving let your requests be made known to God" (Phil. 4:6; also see Col. 4:2). The result of this attitude will be an incomprehensible peace (see Phil. 4:7). Paul's own expressions of gratitude usually included such words as *all, always,* and *everything* (see Phil. 1:3; Col. 1:3; 3:17; 1 Thess. 1:2; 2 Thess. 1:3). Old Testament thanksgiving was to be total, of all the being, for all of God's works. Four times in the psalms the psalmist declared, "I will give thanks to the Lord with all my heart" (Pss. 9:1; 111:1; also see 86:12; 138:1). In the first of these the parallel consequent phrase declares, "I will tell of all Thy wonders."

Gratitude indicates a relationship between source and receiver. In our prayers gratitude indicates one of the most important aspects of our relationship with God. Gratitude acknowledges a specific kind of relationship. Part of Israel's failure in the desert was its failure to acknowledge God. Moses cried, "Do ye thus requite [repay] the Lord, O foolish people and unwise?" (Deut. 32:6, KJV). Only when the particular relationship of giver to receiver is acknowledged properly can the relationship grow.

Gratitude indicates a relationship between the source of good—God—and the receiver of good—people.[6]

Thanksgiving is rejoicing in what God declares to be good.

On pages 52–53 you listed things for which David praised God in Psalm 103. Review your list. Now make your own list of things to praise and thank God for. Include God's attributes and what He has done for you.

_____	_____
_____	_____
_____	_____
_____	_____

Now stop and pray a prayer of adoration, using your list.

Prayers of Intercession

After hallowing God's name, the Model Prayer takes up bringing the kingdom and accomplishing God's will (see Matt. 6:10). The New Testament is full of intercessory prayer that does just that. Intercessory prayer, or prayer on behalf of others, reaches its highest power and its highest goal when it is intended to bring the kingdom and accomplish God's will. Accomplishing God's will, in fact, is the purpose of all prayer. The greatest example not only of intercessory prayer but also of prayer to bring God's kingdom is Jesus' prayer in John 17. Just as He prayed for Peter (see Luke 22:32), He prayed for His disciples in John 17, and in verse 20 He indicated that He was praying for all disciples in all times.

Christ is our example in intercessory prayer.

Christ is our example in intercessory prayer. The work He began on earth He continues through all time. He now appears in God's presence for us (see Heb. 9:24) and always lives to make intercession for those who draw near to God (see Heb. 7:25). Paul developed one of the most poignant expressions of the loving and propitious attitude of our Intercessor: "Who will bring a charge against God's elect? God is the one who justifies; who is the one who condemns? Christ Jesus is He who died, yes, rather who was raised, who is at the right hand of God, who also intercedes for us" (Rom. 8:33-34).

Believers are also taught to pray for one another. Mutual intercession was widely practiced in the New Testament church. James commanded, "Confess your sins to one another, and pray for one another, so that you may be healed. The effective prayer of a righteous man can accomplish much" (Jas. 5:16). The prayer of the Jerusalem church for Peter in Acts 12:5 accomplished much in his release from prison. Paul requested the prayers of the Thessalonians (see 1 Thess. 5:25), and he even asked the Roman church "to strive together with me in your prayers to God for me" (Rom. 15:30). The word Paul used means *to strive with* and indicates that Paul expected them to be earnest in prayer for him.

The scope of the intercessory prayers recorded in the New Testament is almost inexhaustible. Paul prayed for the churches to be spiritually enlightened (see Eph. 1:15-20), know God's will, walk worthy of Him, bear fruit, and be strengthened (see Col. 1: 9-11; also see Phil. 1:9; 1 Thess. 3:10-13; 2 Thess. 1:11). He prayed that they comprehend the love of Christ in order to be filled with the fullness of God (see Eph. 3:14-19) and that their sanctification and preservation be complete (see 1 Thess. 5:23). Each of these prayers is so instructive that it merits extended study.

Paul also requested the prayers of the churches. He asked the Ephesians to pray for him to have bold utterance (see Eph. 6:19), and he asked the Colossians to pray for him to speak with boldness and clarity (see Col. 4:4-5). He requested the Thessalonians, "Pray for us that the word of the Lord may spread rapidly and be glorified … and that we may be delivered from perverse and evil men" (2 Thess. 3:1-2). Paul was so confident in the power of their prayers that he associated his work with their prayers as a joint catalyst in accomplishing God's will. He expected them to be thankful for the answers to their prayers for him: "… you also joining in helping us through your prayers, that thanks may be given by many persons on our behalf for the favor bestowed upon us through the prayers of many" (2 Cor. 1:11). He expressed confidence that the prayers of the Philippian church would accomplish his deliverance from prison (see Phil 1:19).

In the Bible God gives us the following guidelines for prayers of intercession (which also apply to prayers of petition).

Ask in the Spirit. "Pray in the Spirit on all occasions" (Eph. 6:18). This means that every request proceeds from the mind of the Spirit, not from selfish motives or self-serving

"May the God of peace Himself sanctify you entirely; and may your spirit and soul and body be preserved complete, without blame at the coming of our Lord Jesus Christ" (1 Thess. 5:23).

ends. Praying in the Spirit is directly related to praying according to His will.

Ask according to His will. Our weakness in prayer is this: "We do not know what we ought to pray for, but the Spirit himself intercedes for us … in accordance with God's will" (Rom. 8: 26-27). We are to ask according to God's will with the help of the Holy Spirit. When we don't know what to ask, we should keep praying and seeking God's direction for our prayers.

Ask with the mind. "I will also pray with my mind" (1 Cor. 14:15). Our mind helps us form our requests and makes them precise and specific. This is one reason to list prayer requests in a notebook. A prayer list keeps our mind from wandering as we pray and enables us to pray specifically and persistently until the answer comes.

Ask in Jesus' name. " 'You may ask me for anything in my name, and I will do it' " (John 14:14). When we use Jesus' name, we claim to represent Him and act like Him—to have His desires, qualities, gratitude, and outlook. When we prepare to make a request, we should first ask ourselves, *What would Jesus want in this situation?* His desires should become our desires. Praying in Jesus' name also relates to praying according to His will.

Ask while abiding in Christ. Read Jesus' words in the margin. Prayer is both a means and a result of abiding in Christ. To abide in Him, we continue in constant fellowship with Him, we pray without ceasing, and we obediently accept His will and word for us. As a branch abides in the vine, a Christian abides in Christ. We should spend time with Him in prayer and in His Word.

> *" 'If you remain in me and my words remain in you, ask whatever you wish, and it will be given to you' " (John 15:7).*

Ask in faith. " 'Have faith in God. Whatever you ask for in prayer, believe that you have received it, and it will be yours' " (Mark 11:22,24). Asking in faith means asking without doubt in our heart. We should believe that the things we ask will come to pass. We should reflect God's character in always being the same. We should recognize God's authority and power to answer in the way He chooses. We should have confidence in God's care and purposes for our life. Finally, we can claim a God-given Bible promise and anticipate God's response.

Ask in humility. " 'If my people, who are called by my name, will humble themselves and pray …' " (2 Chron. 7:14). Praying in humility recognizes our need of God. Humility submits to God, whereas pride, arrogance, and independence prevent an attitude of humility.

The secret to humility is to understand who God is. Pride always indicates that we have failed to perceive His greatness. We should come to God recognizing His greatness and our need.

Ask in sincerity. When we pray in sincerity, our faith leads us to pray genuine, heartfelt prayers. We are so serious about our praying that our prayer is earnest and fervent, not fake or artificial.

Ask with perseverance. "Pray in the Spirit on all occasions with all kinds of prayers and requests. With this in mind, be alert and always keep on praying for all the saints" (Eph. 6:18). *Perseverance* means *persistence, not giving up.* God expects us to persevere in prayer to make us sure of what He wants and of what we want. He wants to train us to take our eyes off discouraging circumstances and to focus on Him. He also wants us to prove and establish earnestness and to demonstrate real faith.[7]

There are two main results of our prayers of intercession. The first accomplishment of skilled intercession is that it places the intercessor in the position Christ Himself is in. Christ intercedes for us in heaven (see Heb. 7:25), and He intercedes for persons we pray for. Our job is to know His mind. We can know His mind if we constantly depend on Him, study His life, and appeal to the Spirit to lead us that way. Sometimes I pray about an object for weeks before I am able to discern the mind of Christ. But persistence pays off, and ultimately, I begin to feel confident in knowing the mind of the Lord.

The second accomplishment of intercession is that it secures the work of God. God could perfectly well do His work without our prayers, but that is not the way He likes to do it. A love so vast and inclusive that it will not work apart from the participating work of His beloved is inconceivable to us. But can you imagine what working with God does for us (see 2 Cor. 6:1)? It leads us first into identification with His purposes and then into identification with God Himself.[9]

"My own conversion is the result of prayer, long, affectionate, earnest, importunate. Parents prayed for me; God heard their cries, and here I am to preach the Gospel."[8]
—*Charles Haddon Spurgeon (1834–92), pastor of Metropolitan Tabernacle; London, England*

🙢❧🙠

On the following page, make an intercessory prayer list. Include persons you know who are sick or have other problems; family members; church leaders; unsaved persons; local, state, and national leaders; military personnel; nations; those who are hurting and suffering; and missionaries.

_____   _____

_____   _____

_____   _____

_____   _____

Spend time in intercessory prayer, using your list.

Prayers of Petition

The next request in the Model Prayer is " 'Give us this day our daily bread' " (Matt. 6:11). Not only are we encouraged to pray for one another, but we are also told again and again that we may make personal petitions to the Lord. The prayers mentioned in the preceding section are sublimely spiritual in nature, but prayers of petition include everyday physical needs, indicating that the Lord considers our physical needs important enough to pray about. Petition is an important part of our prayer life.

Petition is asking for ourselves, our family, our church, or our group. You might think that the great prayer warriors of the Bible did not emphasize personal petition. Yet many of them made personal petitions. In Genesis 15:2 Abram (later Abraham) asked God for a son. In 1 Samuel 1:10-11 Hannah prayed for a son. King Hezekiah was dying and prayed to live (see 2 Kings 20:1-3). Zechariah and Elizabeth prayed for a child (see Luke 1:13). God heard and answered all of these personal petitions.

The examples in the Bible indicate that God is pleased to hear our personal requests. God's purpose in encouraging petition is to mold us into a certain kind of person. The persons above were in the process of becoming a more godly person. Abraham didn't just receive a son; God gave him a nation. Hannah was becoming a certain kind of person when she prayed for a son, for motherhood changes the character of a woman of God. Hezekiah became one of Israel's greatest kings.

In the case of personal petition above, not only the person but also God's work and kingdom benefited. Abraham's prayer resulted in the chosen race that would prepare the way for Christ. Hannah's prayer gave to Israel Samuel—a great judge and prophet.

"To ask implies a sense of need. ... Seeking means asking plus effort. ... Knocking is asking plus effort plus persistence."[10]
—Clovis A. Chappell (1882–1972), Methodist pastor

Because he did not die, Hezekiah lived to father Manasseh. In so doing, he preserved the messianic line of David that led to the birth of Jesus.[11]

In the Sermon on the Mount Jesus taught us to ask, seek, and knock (see Matt. 7:7-8). Jesus was specifying three attitudes that should characterize our prayers of petition.

Dependence. Throughout the Gospels the numerous requests to Christ for healing are examples of asking. Asking indicates dependence, like, for example, the dependence of a child on his parents. Jesus, in fact, immediately after enjoining us to ask, gave the encouraging example of a father anxious to give good gifts to his son and indicated that the Heavenly Father is immeasurably more willing to give than an earthly father is (see Matt. 7:11). Asking, therefore, suggests the humility of dependence on the petitioner's part and willingness on God's part.

Earnestness. Seeking suggests yearning, earnestness, and effort. Nicodemus was a seeker (see John 3). Isaiah urged that we "seek the Lord while He may be found" (Isa. 55:6). Jesus told us to " 'seek first His kingdom and His righteousness' " (Matt. 6:33). Paul wrote, "Keep seeking the things above" (Col. 3:1). We are to seek not only our own good but also that of our neighbor (see 1 Cor. 10:24).

Persistence. Knocking suggests persistence or, as the Bible puts it, importunity. Jacob's night-long wrestling with God is an example of persistence (see Gen. 32:24-29). Strangely, the Bible speaks more of the Lord's knocking on our door than of our knocking on His (see Luke 12:36; Rev. 3:20); He is persistent in His wooing of us. Because the word Jesus used for *knock* indicates a knock to gain admission, the suggestion is that the kingdom contains many opportunities to which Christians may be admitted.

All three attitudes should permeate prayers of petition. The pronouns in Matthew 7:7 are all plural; the potential of prayer with others has yet to be explored by the home and the church. Interestingly, the assurance of God's answer is stated in the singular, and it is comprehensive (see Matt. 7:8).

" 'Ask, and it shall be given to you; seek, and you shall find; knock, and it shall be opened to you. For everyone who asks receives, and he who seeks finds, and to him who knocks it shall be opened' " (Matt. 7:7-8).

✦

Jesus specified three attitudes in Matthew 7:7 that should characterize our praying. Beside each attitude write why it is important to prayer.

Dependence: _____

_____

Earnestness: _____

_____

Persistence: _____

_____

"Almighty God, we make our earnest prayer that you will keep the United States in your holy protection."[12]
—*George Washington (1732–99), first President of the United States*

One of the most important biblical petitions is the frequently repeated prayer for strength in God's service. The most eloquent of several examples of this is given in Acts 4:24-31. It may have been spoken by Peter, but the church agreed "with one accord" (v. 24). The prayer began with a quotation from Psalm 2, a messianic psalm, equating the resistance of the Jerusalem priests to the new Christian movement with that of the rulers "against the Lord and against His Anointed" (v. 2) in the psalm. One reason for the rapid expansion of the New Testament church was the frequency of the repetition of this prayer for boldness of proclamation and strength in God's service (see Eph. 3:16; 6:19; Col. 1:11; 4:3; 2 Thess. 2:17).

Petition is to be presented without anxiety and with thanksgiving (see Phil. 4:6); Paul assured the Philippian church that God would supply all needs "according to His riches in glory in Christ Jesus" (Phil. 4:19). The result of this kind of prayer will be that "the peace of God, which surpasses all comprehension, shall guard your hearts and your minds in Christ Jesus" (Phil. 4:7). The reasonableness of this is seen in the presence of the God of peace in the lives of those who obey Paul's injunctions (see Phil. 4:9).

On the following page, make a list of petitions for yourself that you would like to pray about. Your list may include physical needs, such as health, finance, or work. It may include emotional and spiritual needs. It may include some of the deepest desires of your heart that are known only to you and God.

_____ _____

_____ _____

_____ _____

_____ _____

Now stop and spend time praying for yourself, using your list.

Prayers of Repentance

After the prayer for daily sustenance Jesus told us to ask for the forgiveness of our sins (see Matt. 6:12). A Christian is not asking for a legal cancellation of sin, of course, for the cross cancels the legal debt of our sin. But constant agreement with God about the nature of sin is the only way we can maintain fellowship with Him in His holiness.

God is holy. He is separate, pure, and righteous. God reveals His holiness because He wants you to be holy as He is holy: "It is written: 'Be holy, because I am holy' " (1 Pet. 1:16, NIV). Yet we cannot be holy apart from God's work in us.

When God revealed Himself to persons in biblical accounts, one of the first qualities they recognized was His holiness. Isaiah went into the temple when king Uzziah died. Even though the earthly king was dead, Isaiah saw that God had not vacated His throne. Read in the margin what happened.

Confronted with God's holiness and purity, Isaiah cried out because of his sin. He agreed with what God already knew to be true. Isaiah had no reason to feel pride. God responded in love by taking away Isaiah's sin. Isaiah was cleansed and forgiven.[13]

John wrote, "If we confess our sins, He is faithful and righteous to forgive us our sins and to cleanse us from all unrighteousness" (1 John 1:9). The word for _confess_ literally means _to say the same thing_ and implies agreement with another. Confession is not just admitting our sins to God; He never needs information. Rather, confession is aligning ourselves in attitude with Him. Sin grieves us in our new nature in the same way (but not to the same extent) that it grieves God. When I sin, I do not tell God, "I admit that I

"I saw the Lord seated on a throne. ... Above him were seraphs. ... And they were calling to one another:
" 'Holy, holy, holy
_   is the Lord Almighty;_
the whole earth is full
_   of his glory.'_
_   " 'Woe to me!' I cried._
'I am ruined! For I am a man of unclean lips, and I live among a people of unclean lips, and my eyes have seen the King, the Lord Almighty.'
_   "Then one of the seraphs flew to me with a live coal in his hand, which he had taken with tongs from the altar. With it he touched my mouth and said, 'See, this has touched your lips; your guilt is taken away and your sin atoned for' "_
(Isa. 6:1-3,5-7, NIV).

sinned," but rather, I tell Him that I agree with Him about the nature of my action. In doing so, I align myself with His attitude toward my sin.

Forgiving others. When we pray to God, we should pray only in accord with what we know of His character, and this is in accord with Jesus' command that we ask for forgiveness " 'as we also have forgiven our debtors' " (Matt. 6:12). God's mercy is limitless, and Jesus answered Peter's question about our limit on forgiveness by saying that we should forgive " 'up to seventy times seven' " (Matt. 18:22). There must be no limit to our forgiveness, just as there is no limit to God's. Jesus illustrated His command to Peter with the story of a slave who was forgiven by his king but would not himself forgive others (see Matt. 18:23-35). We are not to be like the slave; we are to be like the king in the parable. Jesus' own example is like that of the king. On the cross Jesus prayed, " 'Father, forgive them; for they do not know what they are doing' " (Luke 23:34). We are to have the mind of Christ (see 1 Cor. 2:16).

> *"Weeping, mourning (repenting), fasting and praying before our God is the greatest need we have today."*[14]
> —James T. Draper Jr., president, LifeWay Christian Resources

Many Christians associate forgiveness with feelings and therefore struggle to change inner feelings. But forgiveness is an action, legal in nature. Stephen's example is instructive. Compare his dying prayer to that of Jesus. As Stephen was dying, he prayed, " 'Lord, do not hold this sin against them!' " (Acts. 7:60). Paul wrote, "Never take your own revenge, beloved, but leave room for the wrath of God, for it is written, 'Vengeance is Mine, I will repay, says the Lord' " (Rom. 12:19).

Forgiveness, then, is simply placing all aspects of our case in God's hands, turning it over to God, as Stephen did. We give it to our Defender, who says that revenge is His own prerogative. It frees God to work in the lives of those who hurt us, according to His wisdom and His pleasure rather than our changing whims. It is likely that the conversion of Saul of Tarsus, who watched Stephen die, had at least some root in Stephen's remarkable prayer. Much of Jesus' teaching on forgiveness was in connection with prayer. It is in prayer, in fellowship with God, that we best demonstrate His character, as Stephen did.

Receiving God's forgiveness. It is as imperative that we accept forgiveness from God as it is that we forgive others. The Bible again and again gives a picture of infinite divine forgiveness, sometimes with graphic language and picturesque figures to help us understand the greatness of God's mercy. Micah said that when

God forgives us, He casts our sins "into the depths of the sea" (Mic. 7:19). Isaiah described it as wiping out our transgressions and quoted the Lord as saying that He would not remember our sins (see Isa. 43:25). He quoted a writing of Hezekiah: "Thou hast cast all my sins behind Thy back" (Isa. 38:17).

But supremely, it was the New Testament that gave us the most adequate picture of the perfect cancellation of forgiven sin. The writer of Hebrews asked, "If the blood of goats and bulls and the ashes of a heifer sprinkling those who have been defiled, sanctify for the cleansing of the flesh, how much more will the blood of Christ, who through the eternal Spirit offered Himself without blemish to God, cleanse your conscience from dead works to serve the living God?" (Heb. 9:13-14).

A young woman once called me in deep remorse over sin in her life. She believed in God's forgiveness yet felt unclean. I asked her, "If the blood of Christ is what cleanses you, how clean are you?" God's forgiveness is absolute. All His actions, like His attributes, are absolutes. The Keil and Delitzsch translation of Lamentations 3:22-23 gives a picture of mercy so unfailing that it is ever new: "[It is a sign of] the mercies of Jahveh that we are not consumed, for His compassions fail not; [they are] new every morning: great is Thy faithfulness."[15] Repeatedly, God's mercies or lovingkindnesses are described as infinite or as multitudinous (see Ps. 89:2; Isa. 63:7), and the measure of God's forgiveness is not our feelings but His great compassion (see Ps. 51:1). God's compassions are renewed daily!

God's forgiveness is absolute.

Newness is the law of the kingdom, and *new* is one of the most important words in the New Testament. Newness characterizes not only God's compassions but also our walk in newness of life (see Rom. 6:4). Paul encouraged all Christians of history with his word "If any man is in Christ, he is a new creature; the old things passed away; behold, new things have come" (2 Cor. 5:17). Forgiven sin, the old, is in the past and is to be put there; it has passed away.

◖◖◖❀◗◗◗

Consider areas of your life in which you need to ask God's forgiveness. Recall words you have spoken, things you have done or failed to do, and thoughts. On the following page, make a list to pray about.

_____   _____

_____   _____

_____   _____

Stop and pray a prayer of forgiveness, using your list.

Spend a few minutes reading Psalm 103:12; Isaiah 43:25; Micah 7:19; and 1 John 1:9 in your Bible. Summarize in one sentence what God does when we repent and seek His forgiveness.

_____

_____

Now strike through everything you wrote in your prayer list above. This symbolizes God's cleansing and removing your sins. Pray again, this time thanking God for His cleansing and forgiveness.

Prayers of Deliverance

After the plea for forgiveness in the Model Prayer comes a prayer for deliverance from evil (see Matt. 6:13). The word for *evil* here could be either neuter—evil in general—or masculine—that is, Satan. Jesus used the same word in Matthew 13:19,38 to refer to Satan, as did Paul in Ephesians 6:16. In either case, the injunction to pray for deliverance from evil implies that deliverance is God's will and may be secured through prayer.

Deliverance from temptation. Our protection from temptation is important to Jesus. Later, He Himself asked on our behalf this petition: " 'I do not ask Thee to take them out of the world, but to keep them from the evil one' " (John 17:15). The same night He prayed this prayer, He urged the disciples to " 'pray that you may not enter into temptation' " (Luke 22:40). Repetition of the injunction lends weight to its importance.

"As far as the east is from the west, So far has He removed our transgressions from us" (Ps. 103:12).

68

❧

Think about areas of your life in which you are especially susceptible to temptation. Make a list of things from which to ask God's protection.

_____   _____

_____   _____

_____   _____

_____   _____

Spend a few minutes praying for God to protect you and to keep you from the evil one.

Now read 1 Corinthians 10:13 from your Bible.

The protection God gives is effective; John wrote about a sure confidence: "We know that no one who is born of God sins; but He [Christ] who was born of God keeps him and the evil one does not touch him" (1 John 5:18). Paul gave the same assurance: "The Lord is faithful, and He will strengthen and protect you from the evil one" (2 Thess. 3:3). He assured Timothy, "The Lord will deliver me from every evil deed, and will bring me safely to His heavenly kingdom" (2 Tim. 4:18). Peter echoed the same idea: "The Lord knows how to rescue the godly from temptation" (2 Pet. 2:9). The most decisive and unquestionable assurance of deliverance in the New Testament, after Jesus' injunction, is Paul's rather bold statement "No temptation has overtaken you but such as is common to man; and God is faithful, who will not allow you to be tempted beyond what you are able, but with the temptation will provide the way of escape also, that you may be able to endure it" (1 Cor. 10:13).

Protection. A Christian may ask for general protection and safety. The names by which God is called in the psalter—Shield, Fortress, Refuge—indicate an ancient, rocklike faith in God's keeping power. The writers of the Old Testament repeatedly assured us of safety and protection under Yahweh:

"Call upon Me in the day of trouble; I shall rescue you" (Ps. 50:15).

I have set the Lord continually before me;
Because He is at my right hand, I will not be shaken (Ps. 16:8).

He will give His angels charge concerning you,
To guard you in all your ways (Ps. 91:11).

The Lord is your keeper;
The Lord is your shade on your right hand (Ps. 121:5).

Every word of God is tested;
He is a shield to those who take refuge in Him (Prov. 30:5).

The eyes of the Lord move to and fro throughout the earth that He may strongly support those whose heart is completely His (2 Chron. 16:9; Hanani the seer was speaking to Asa when Asa refused to rely on the Lord).

"Satan despises prayer. ... He does all he can to keep us from praying. When we pray we are fighting against the rulers of darkness. But Satan dreads prayer. ... Though Satan laughs at prayerless toil and mocks at human wisdom, he trembles when Christians pray."[16]
—*R. G. Lee (1886–1978), pastor of Bellevue Baptist Church; Memphis, Tennessee; and president of the Southern Baptist Convention, 1948–51*

In chapter 1 you identified several prayers with the persons who prayed them. The same prayers are found below and on the following page. This time classify each prayer according to the five kinds of prayer you studied in this chapter. Beside each prayer, write the letter corresponding to the correct kind.

____ 1. "Father, forgive them; for they do not know what they are doing." (Jesus)

____ 2. "Jesus, Son of David, have mercy on me!" (Bartimaeus)

____ 3. "Wash me thoroughly from my iniquity, and cleanse me from my sin. ... Against Thee, Thee only, I have sinned." (David)

____ 4. "There is no one holy like the Lord, indeed, there is no one besides Thee, nor is there any rock like our God." (Hannah)

a. adoration
b. intercession
c. petition
d. repentance
e. deliverance

___ 5. "I do not ask Thee to take them out of the world, but to keep them from the evil one." (Jesus)

___ 6. "If Thou wilt, forgive their sin—and if not, please blot me out from Thy book which Thou hast written!" (Moses)

___ 7. "Lord, do not hold this sin against them!" (Stephen)

___ 8. "Depart from me, for I am a sinful man." (Peter)

___ 9. "Father, if it is possible, let this cup pass from Me; yet not as I will, but as Thou wilt." (Jesus)

___ 10. "Blessed be the God and Father of our Lord Jesus Christ, who has blessed us with every spiritual blessing." (Paul)

___ 11. "O Lord my God, in Thee I have taken refuge; save me from all those who pursue me, and deliver me." (David)

The forms of prayer suggested by the Model Prayer are limited only by our imagination and should be amplified by study of all the prayers of the Bible. In all of them we identify with God and are being brought increasingly into His image. Whatever form of prayer we use, our hearts and minds remain in agreement with Him and His purposes in all circumstances and in all times. Prayer is fellowship with God and is successful only to the degree that it is in agreement with Him.

❦❦❦

Go back to four of the five prayer lists you have made: adoration, intercession, petition, and deliverance from temptation. If you do not already have a prayer notebook, begin one by transferring the four lists into it.

Do not go to your repentance prayer list. Those things are gone, and God does not remember them. Instead,

*I must tell Jesus
all of my trials;
I cannot bear these
burdens alone;
In my distress He kindly
will help me;
He ever loves and cares
for His own.*

*I must tell Jesus
all of my troubles;
He is a kind, compas-
sionate friend;
If I but ask Him,
He will deliver,
Make of my troubles
quickly an end.*

*Tempted and tried, I need
a great Savior,
One who can help my
burdens to bear;
I must tell Jesus, I must
tell Jesus;
He all my cares and
sorrows will share.*

*I must tell Jesus! I must
tell Jesus!
I cannot bear my burdens
alone;
I must tell Jesus! I must
tell Jesus!
Jesus can help me,
Jesus alone.*[17]

add to your notebook a blank page titled "Repentance" so that you can record anything in the future for which you need to ask forgiveness. Cultivate the habit of praying regularly with these five kinds of prayers. Keep a record of answers to your prayers.

[1]Matthew Henry, in *All the Promises of the Bible* by Herbert Lockyer (Grand Rapids: Zondervan, 1962), 147.

[2]W. A. Criswell, *Great Doctrines of the Bible* (Grand Rapids: Zondervan, 1986), 28.

[3]T. W. Hunt and Catherine Walker, *Disciple's Prayer Life* (Nashville: LifeWay Press, 1997), 80–81.

[4]Adapted from Hunt and Walker, *Disciple's Prayer Life,* 79.

[5]T. W. Hunt and Claude V. King, *In God's Presence* (Nashville: LifeWay Press, 1995), 44.

[6]Hunt and Walker, *Disciple's Prayer Life,* 65.

[7]Adapted from Hunt and King, *In God's Presence,* 57–58.

[8]Charles Haddon Spurgeon, in *Great Preaching on Prayer,* comp. Curtis Hutson (Murfreesboro, TN: Sword of the Lord Publisher, 1988), 55.

[9]T. W. Hunt, "The Basics of Prayer," in *A House of Prayer,* comp. John Franklin (Nashville: LifeWay Press, 2000), 9.

[10]Clovis G Chappell, *Preaching on the Words of Jesus* (Grand Rapids: Baker Books, 1996), 195, 200, 202.

[11]Hunt and King, *In God's Presence,* 65.

[12]George Washington, in *The One-Year Book of Personal Prayer* (Wheaton, IL: Tyndale House, 1991), July 4.

[13]Adapted from Hunt and King, *In God's Presence,* 38.

[14]James T. Draper Jr., *Facts & Trends,* December 2001, 3.

[15]C. F. Keil and F. Delitzsch, *Commentary on the Old Testament in 10 Volumes,* VIII (Grand Rapids: William B. Eerdmans Publishing Company, n.d.), 401.

[16]R. G. Lee, *The Bible and Prayer* (Nashville: Convention Press, 1950), 35.

[17]Elisha A. Hoffman, "I Must Tell Jesus," in *The Baptist Hymnal* (Nashville: Convention Press, 1991), 455.

Answers to matching activity on pages 70–71: 1. b, 2. c, 3. d, 4. a, 5. b, e, 6. b, 7. b, 8. d, 9. c, 10. a, 11. e

Chapter 4
Answers to Questions About Prayer

The Scriptures and experience are intended to encourage us to pray, but many Christians feel a vague reluctance to pray. This reluctance may be rooted in uncertainties in their minds. Uncertainty is the enemy of faith. It is better to face our questions squarely, to accept the verdict of Scripture, and to move forward into the kind of prayer that pleases God and accomplishes His will.

If God Already Knows Everything, Why Should We Pray?

There can be no question that God knows everything. Certainly our loving Father desires the fellowship, not the silence, of His children. The real questions, therefore, are what is prayer, and what does it do?

Of the beings of higher intelligence, the Bible names only two orders—humankind and angels. That the angels were created is clear (see Neh. 9:6; Col. 1:16). Like humanity, they were made. The fact that they are spiritual in nature (see Heb. 1:14) and powerful (see Ps. 103:20) leads many people to believe that they are eternally superior to humanity in rank.

Nevertheless, the Bible pictures redeemed humanity as presently in training for a future reign that will be superior to all other revealed orders of creation. Ultimately, we are to be superior in authority and rank to the angels themselves. It was Adam, not an angel, who was made in God's image and was granted dominion over animal life (see Gen. 1:26), but Adam fell and spoiled God's plan for him. The second Adam, Jesus Christ, did not fall and, as representative Man, removed the curse of the law necessitated by the first Adam's fall (see Gal. 3:13). Christ accomplished the possibility of a return to "the image of the heavenly" (1 Cor. 15:49) for the human race.

Certainly our loving Father desires the fellowship, not the silence, of His children.

73

What is involved in the achievement of this second Adam? Even in their present earthly life the authority of the followers who accept His new life exceeds all imagination. We are redeemed and forgiven (see Eph. 1:7), born eternally of imperishable seed (see 1 Pet. 1:23), and are now children of God (see Rom. 8:16). As such, we have the mind of Christ Himself (see 1 Cor. 2:16), are conformed to His image (see Rom. 8:29), and therefore bear "the image of the heavenly" (1 Cor. 15:49). In this new and secure position we bear a regal authority. Paul wrote the Corinthian church, "All things belong to you" (1 Cor. 3:22).

"If we endure, we shall also reign with Him" (2 Tim. 2:12).

The future of this new humanity is even more exalted and noble. We are joint heirs with Christ, who is the heir of all things (see Heb. 1:2), and will be glorified with Him (see Rom. 8:17). We are to reign with Him (see 2 Tim. 2:12; also see Luke 22:29-30; Rom. 5:17; Rev. 20:6) and therefore are the ultimate and cosmic nobility of eternity. It is somewhat frightening that we will also sit in judgment on angels (see 1 Cor. 6:3)—surely an awesome authority hardly conceivable at the present! So great is the destiny of God's children that creation is expectantly longing for the unveiling of the identity of the sons of God (see Rom. 8:19)!

If you were God, bringing His children to that high state, how would you do it? The children of earthly kings around the world are trained in the ways of nobility from infancy. They participate in the privileges of royalty, learn the courtesies of the court, are trained in the interaction of various offices and authorities, carefully study the responsibilities of their present and future office, and assume such responsibilities as their age will allow. Their relation to the ruling monarch is expected to be responsible. They are royal from birth and are expected to act like it.

Much of this description of children of earthly monarchs is consistent with the Bible's description of the nature and work of the future rulers of the universe. Our work is royal work; we are actually workers together with God (see 2 Cor. 6:1). Our nature is like the Sovereign's; we are His children. It is His court, and the responsibilities are spelled out by His Word.

Most important of all the work is spiritual work. Spiritual work can be accomplished only with spiritual methods, and the only mover in any spiritual project must be God Himself. How do we cooperate with God in this work? The answer is obviously prayer. This is why the Bible places so much emphasis on prayer. Prayer is an awesome, regal responsibility, carrying with it great accountability but also possibilities of vast accomplishment.

God could move on His own. He can take the initiative, as He did in creation and redemption. He needs no permission to act. And yet, dealing with His children, it was His wisdom to place them in a training ground appropriate to their learning processes. We are to govern, but we presently exist in an environment containing spiritual elements hostile to His sovereignty. What else could be better training?

This is why in everything we are to present our requests with thanksgiving to God (see Phil. 4:6). Nothing is excluded, because all things affect the progress of the kingdom. Our work is large, and our faith operates across that part of God's sovereignty that is visible to us. The long list of things we should pray for in the Bible (for governors, for churches, for boldness) brings the entire movement of humankind, government, churches, and the kingdom under the influence of our prayers.

God could move without our cooperation. But our cooperation is the method God uses to demonstrate His sovereignty. All power derives from God; He is the most powerful Agent in the universe. Prayer provides a way for us to cooperate with our all-powerful God.

God could work without prayer. Some of God's work is done unilaterally. The might, glory, and power of creation and redemption are beyond our comprehension; we could not have cooperated in them. Creation and redemption are uniquely a divine work, too grand for what we were made to be. But the governing of the universe and the management of the world we know are not beyond us. God has chosen to bring us in on that governing process because of our eternal work of reigning that is ahead of us.

At times we cannot see this grand picture because our minds become befuddled by our sins, blemishes, and various imperfections. We cannot see the forest for the trees, and we cannot see the trees for the moss, rocks, and grass. But the forest, the grand picture, is there. It is quite clear in Scripture.

So in prayer we ask. At times we get outside the bounds of His plan and ask for the wrong thing or ask from wrong motives. We must learn, and we can learn even from our mistakes. This is what we are now doing. How does a ruler rule? We must go through God's process.

Prayer provides a way for us to cooperate with our all-powerful God.

75

Sometimes we seek. But not all is appropriate for a spiritual kingdom or for a holy God. At times our seeking becomes groping because that is the only way we can learn to seek in the right manner. Sometimes we seem to stumble on the right answer and delight in our progress.

At times we knock. Not all opportunities are proper for royalty, but many are, and living as we are, with the mind of Christ, in the image of God, representing the interests of the one King, we delight when those noble and right opportunities open up before our earnest progress.

We do not pray to give God information. We pray because of who we are. It is the wise and holy decision of God Himself that the work of His kingdom be advanced through prayer. His choice of method is that we do that most important of all works. He uses us, directs us to pray rightly, and validates His work in us by kingdom progress. We cannot base our spiritual work on our material resources—our own money, strength, or talent. God does not need our resources; all things belong to Him (see Ps. 50:7-12). We need to use all the resources available to us in the power of God Himself—His wisdom, His spiritual way, His will, His might (see Zech. 4:6).

" 'Not by might, nor by power, but by My Spirit,' says the Lord of hosts" (Zech. 4:6).

As you work through this chapter, you will be asked to summarize Dr. Hunt's answer to each question. Doing this will help reinforce your learning and will provide a quick reference for review. Also, you will be equipped to help others who may have the same questions.

Let's do the first one. Answer in your own words: If God already knows everything, why should we pray?

_____

_____

_____

_____

If People Are Free to Make Choices, What Good Is Praying for Others?

This question presents us with the age-old problem of the balance between God's sovereignty and humanity's free will. Quite unmistakably, Jesus affirmed: " 'You did not choose Me, but I chose you, and appointed you, that you should go and bear fruit, and that your fruit should remain, that whatever you ask of the Father in My name, He may give it to you' " (John 15:16). Yet He also invited, " 'Let the one who wishes take the water of life without cost' " (Rev. 22:17). Biblical paradoxes usually open wider the doors of our understanding.

Each of the two statements is reinforced by numerous other references. Jesus clearly chose the twelve (see Luke 6:13). The disciples' understanding of His prerogative to choose is shown in their prayer for Judas's replacement: " 'Thou, Lord, who knowest the hearts of all men, show which one of these two Thou hast chosen' " (Acts 1:24). He told Ananias, who was doubting Saul of Tarsus, " 'He is a chosen instrument of Mine' " (Acts 9:15). Yet the rich young ruler had complete freedom to choose his own will, to reject Christ (see Matt. 19:22). The Bible unapologetically presents God's elective freedom to choose whom He will; it also clearly leaves the choice of accepting or rejecting God to the individual.

The dynamic interplay between God's will and human will resembles a divinely directed drama. The initiative is always with God, the response with humanity. God will not violate our freedom of will. Because God does not need anything we can give, like talent or money, the one thing He desires is our will. We are free to give that.

God introduces factors that affect our decision. It may be a dramatic factor, as in Saul's Damascus-road experience. It may be a stated condition, as in the case of the rich young ruler. These factors may be introduced by our prayers. My wife and I once prayed three years for a lost man. We were encouraged because we noticed obvious indications that the Holy Spirit was bringing him under uncomfortable conviction. After three years he finally accepted Christ, but today, in retrospect, the backward look at those years of prayer is a fascinating study of the interplay between the Holy Spirit's will and the man's positive and negative reaction to it. He was free, and God was free. Persistent prayer finally found the point at which he surrendered his life.

God will not violate our freedom of will.

The fact that so many in the Bible rejected God or even rebelled against Him proves that God did not force them into decisions. The fact that so many followed Him proves that the will can cooperate with God. In any case, both God's will and human will remain free. This truth gives glory to the drama of redemption.

Answer in your own words: If people are free to make choices, what good is praying for others?

____

____

____

For What Is It Proper to Pray?

"Be anxious for nothing, but in everything by prayer and supplication with thanksgiving let your requests be made known to God" (Phil. 4:6).

The answer to this question is stated without hesitation in Philippians 4:6: pray about everything. Miss Bertha Smith was a legendary missionary to China for many years. Prayer and faith characterized her life. In her retirement years she traveled widely to encourage Christians to pray and believe God. Miss Bertha once had a busy schedule planned for the next day but could not go to sleep that night because of mosquitoes buzzing about. She swatted them for a while, but when reinforcements came, matters grew worse. Suddenly she sat up from her cot and said matter-of-factly: "Lord, if I'm going to work for You tomorrow, You've got to do something about these bugs! I've got to have some rest." Miss Bertha could talk to God like that. She, like Abraham and Moses, was God's friend and would talk with God the way God talked with Moses: "The Lord used to speak to Moses face to face, just as a man speaks to his friend" (Ex. 33:11). Miss Bertha lay back down, closed her eyes, and went to sleep as the mosquitoes went home for the night.[1] Horses and chariots of fire can deliver from Benhadad's army (see 2 Kings 6:17); just one angel can defeat an Assyrian army (see 2 Kings 19:35); one angel can shut the mouths of hungry lions (see Dan. 6:22); and God's angels can drive swarming mosquitoes away so that one of His saints can sleep!

Yes, we are to pray about everything. No detail is too small to take to God in prayer. Nothing in the Bible encourages us to divide life into secular and sacred categories. Can you imagine Jesus having His earthly life categorized like that? It is foreign to the Jewish mentality, and no Christian writings reflect such a division. Christianity and Judaism alike hallow all of life as good. Jesus enjoyed eating. He blessed the wedding at Cana, and He enjoyed a variety of wholesome friendships. For Jesus, all of life was good.

However, we should not ask for some things. James 4:1-3 makes it clear that we are not to ask for something in order to spend it solely on our pleasures. We are to pray for God's will and the coming of His kingdom. Several years ago I surveyed the answered prayers in the Bible. Among the patterns I discovered was the fact that most answered prayers were concerned strictly with the advance of the divine work, such as Moses' prayers for the nation advancing through the desert. Fewer of the Bible prayers could be considered personal—such as Hannah's prayer for a son.

None of the personal prayers that were answered contradicted the nature and purposes of the divine work; in fact, they usually enhanced it. For example, Hannah's prayer produced Samuel, a pivotal figure in Israel's history (see 1 Sam. 1:10-20). Some time after my survey of the prayers of the Bible, I documented the answered prayers over a specific time period in my life and was amazed to discover the same proportions emerging: roughly ⅔ of my answered prayers were primarily concerned with the advance of God's kingdom work, and ⅓ were personal—and yet all of the answered personal requests in some significant way accomplished a divine work that helped others and made a contribution to God's work in the church.

There are also inappropriate ways to pray, but these will be discussed in chapter 5.

"Prayer is not simply getting things from God, that is a most initial form of prayer; prayer is getting into perfect communion with God."[2]
—*Oswald Chambers (1874–1917), devotional speaker*

(C·❦·D)

Answer in your own words: For what is it proper to pray?

_____

_____

_____

Does God Hear the Prayers of Non-Christians?

This extremely knotty question will receive different answers from different people, according to how they interpret the biblical information. Here we must concern ourselves with the major, salient, unassailable facts as revealed in the Bible.

Fact 1. God loves all persons, wants them to come to Him, and introduces factors into their lives to bring them to Himself. Naaman was a Syrian, was a non-Jew, and was probably never circumcised, and yet God answered his request for healing through Elisha. As a result, Naaman turned to Yahweh, the God of Israel. He confessed, " 'Behold now, I know that there is no God in all the earth, but in Israel' " (2 Kings 5:15) and declared that in the future he would serve only Yahweh (see v. 17).

Fact 2. Jesus tenderly spoke of God's love for the Gentiles when His townspeople of Nazareth rejected Him. He specifically referred to God's feeding of the widow of Zarephath, in the Gentile region of Phoenicia, through Elijah, and to Naaman's healing. Jesus also healed the daughter of the Syrophoenician woman (see Matt. 15:21-28).

Fact 3. God is free to use Christian, non-Christian, Jew, or Gentile to accomplish His purposes as He sees fit. He used the pagan rulers Nebuchadnezzar (see Dan. 2—4), Darius (see Dan. 6:4-27), and Cyrus (see 2 Chron. 36:22-23). All of these retained their paganism, and in none of these cases is there specific prayer, although Darius's beautiful decree (see Dan. 6:26-27) comes very close. We must recognize, however, God's freedom to use whatever person or factor He wants to use. He even directed the speech of the pagan hireling Baalam (see Num. 23:7-10,18-24).

Fact 4. Israel was given special instructions to love aliens and to include strangers in their national life. Israel was told that God loves aliens and provides for them (see Deut. 10:18-19). One section of the Levitical law provided that aliens in Israel should observe the law (see Num. 15:15-29). Aliens could even elect to become Jews (see Ex. 12:48; also see Gen. 17:27; Deut. 23:8). The psalmist declared that the Lord protects strangers (see Ps. 146:9).

God's omniscience enables Him to hear all human discourse, holy and profane, and all these factors interplay in accomplishing for a loving God the things His tenderness wants to accomplish as

God loves all persons, wants them to come to Him, and introduces factors into their lives to bring them to Himself.

He hears desperate cries from the needy. He loves the widow, the poor, the stranger, and the orphan.

Fact 5. All life and all provision come from God. The psalmist declared,

The eyes of all look to Thee,
And Thou dost give them their food in due time (Ps. 145:15).

Fact 6. The Model Prayer demonstrates the fact that God always puts His business and His purposes ahead of all concerns any of us might have, whether we are Christian or non-Christian. An omnipresent, omnipotent, omniscient God is not too busy to attend to many things, but even God has priorities. A Christian has bases on which to pray that other people do not have. God wants most to hear serious prayer that cooperates with God in accomplishing His purposes. He always gives priority to the bringing of His kingdom.

A Christian has bases on which to pray that other people do not have.

With all of these things in mind, we can conclude that God is sovereign. He is not limited by anything we believe about Him. Simply because He is God, He answers prayer according to His own wisdom.

A Christian is uniquely related to God as His child. God made many promises to answer prayer solely to believers. However, this fact does not limit God in His concern for all people.

Answer in your own words: Does God hear the prayers of non-Christians?

_____

_____

_____

_____

_____

Why Do Christians Pray in Jesus' Name?

At least three different times in His last discourse Jesus told us to offer prayers in His name (see John 14:13-14; 15:16; 16:23-24, 26-27). He said that when His people are gathered in His name, He will be present (see Matt. 18:20).

Jesus' name is our legal authorization for prayer. He is our way to God (see John 14:6), for there is no other name under heaven by which we must be saved (see Acts 4:12).

Jesus' name establishes our identity. Jesus' name is now our name, Christian, and using His name reflects our developing His character. It is not a ritual. The seven sons of Sceva attempted to use Jesus' name outside His character, and the evil spirit they were exorcising overpowered them and wounded them (see Acts 19: 13-17). Jesus' name identifies our association with His family; Paul addressed his first letter to the Corinthian church "to those … who in every place call upon the name of our Lord Jesus Christ" (1 Cor. 1:2).

Jesus' name appropriates all God has done for us in Christ. It acknowledges that our highest, richest possession is our identity with Christ the Beloved. As the beggar pleaded for alms from Peter and John, Peter told him, " 'I do not possess silver and gold, but what I do have I give to you: In the name of Jesus Christ the Nazarene—walk!' " (Acts 3:6).

Jesus' name appropriates all that is in God's revealed character. It places us in the long line of those who have called on the Lord's name through history. At the beginning of prayer history, after the birth of Enosh (man in his weakness), "then men began to call upon the name of the Lord" (Gen. 4:26). When Samuel was comforting Israel after their sin in demanding a king, he assured them, " 'The Lord will not abandon His people on account of His great name' " (1 Sam. 12:22).

Jesus' name is the intensifying agent of unity in the body of Christ. I have seen the power of unity in Christ's name demonstrated many times. At Southwestern Seminary for many years one of my classes always developed a remarkable prayer bond early in the course and saw a large number of unusual and dramatic answers—jobs found, marriages healed, the sick returned to health. I do not know why that course was so honored by the

Jesus' name establishes our identity.

82

Lord, but its special blessing was demonstrated by the fact that graduates often called back to request prayer by that class.

Jesus' name indicates reverence for His divinity. The use and honor of Jesus' name were important to the New Testament churches. Thanksgiving in Ephesus was to be given in His name (see Eph. 5:20). Paul prayed that Jesus' name might be glorified in the church at Thessalonica (see 2 Thess. 1:11-12). The use of Jesus' name is one indication of the centrality of Christ in New Testament times. The name of Yahweh had been important in the Old Testament since the giving of the third commandment (see Ex. 20:7) and continued prominent in the later Old Testament writings (see Deut. 28:58; Ps. 99:3). Jesus began the Model Prayer with the solemn phrase " 'Hallowed be Thy name' " (Matt. 6:9). As revelation unfolded, the church legitimately attached to Jesus' name the traditional reverence it had always exhibited for God's name. That reverence sprang from the biblical revelation itself and remains the basis on which we come to God and on which we offer our prayers.

> *"… always giving thanks for all things in the name of our Lord Jesus Christ to God, even the Father"* *(Eph. 5:20).*

Answer in your own words: Why do Christians pray in Jesus' name?

_____

_____

_____

_____

How Can a Christian Pray Without Ceasing?

Paul wrote in 1 Thessalonians 5:17: "Pray without ceasing." We may wonder how this can be possible. Of course, it is not possible for us to pray orally all the time, but it is possible always to be in a spirit of prayer and continually realize God's presence. Praying without ceasing has two dimensions.

Our prayers should be regular and continuous. Daniel prayed three times every day (see Dan. 6:10). The members of the church in the Book of Acts "continued stedfastly in … prayers" (Acts 2:42, KJV). Paul wrote Timothy, "I have remembrance of thee in my prayers night and day" (2 Tim. 1:3).

Nehemiah was burdened by the state of affairs of the remnant of people living in Jerusalem. He prayed to God in detail (see Neh. 1:5-11). His private praying prepared him for continuing in a state of prayer. When the king gave Nehemiah an invitation to make a request, he "prayed to the God of heaven" (Neh. 2:4, KJV) and made his request. That had to be a brief prayer. Nehemiah wanted God's will accomplished by the king's response. Nehemiah was a man who prayed without ceasing.

Our prayers should reflect a constant attitude of relating everything in life to God every hour of the day. Such constancy is one way to recognize God is every department of our life and in every relationship we have. Paul said that he prayed unceasingly for the Roman and the Colossian churches (see Rom. 1:9; Col. 1:9). Anything in our environment can prompt us to acknowledge God. A beautiful landscape calls for praise; God is its Creator. Any small or large blessing should prompt thanksgiving; an attitude of gratitude recognizes God as the source of all good gifts. Sin should bring forth immediate confession. Need in our life should cause us to turn to God immediately.[3]

Answer in your own words: How can a Christian pray without ceasing?

_____

_____

_____

How Is Fasting Beneficial?

A discipline that has faded from special prayer efforts but has proved effective in the past is fasting. Jesus practiced fasting (see Matt. 4:2), as did Moses (see Ex. 34:28). Jesus' words in Matthew 6:16-18, printed in the margin, indicate that He assumed His followers would occasionally fast.

" 'Whenever you fast, do not put on a gloomy face as the hypocrites do, for they neglect their appearance in order to be seen fasting by men. Truly I say to you, they have their reward in full. But you, when you fast, anoint your head, and wash your face so that you may not be seen fasting by men, but by your Father who is in secret; and your Father who sees in secret will repay you' " (Matt. 6:16-18).

We too may choose to fast from time to time. The value of fasting lies in the concentration of our will on God. In fasting, the will says no to bodily appetites. It affirms that the highest and most worthwhile desires are not physical but spiritual. The will deliberately takes leave of the outer world and directs the mind to God alone. That is why fasting and praying go together.

Fasting is best undertaken when we are free from duties and other cares and can concentrate on prayer. Often it is wise to be alone. Both Moses and Jesus were alone when they fasted. Fasting may be done jointly with a spouse or friend(s), especially if the prayer accompanying it is for a special concern to all involved. Fasting may be undertaken for many kinds of special prayer efforts, such as for a revival, for a need, or simply for the discipline of concentrating on God.

A fast may be partial or complete. A partial fast, for example, may include drinking water or fruit juice but avoiding solid food. A fast may be for any length of time and may include one missed meal or many. Most fasts of more than one meal should begin with the evening meal. Fasting denies the body blood sugar and should not be undertaken if a person has any physical abnormality or illness, especially diabetes or hypoglycemia. To fast when involved in heavy physical or mental work is not wise, either.

Jesus instructed us not to allow any outward signs to be seen when we fast (see Matt. 6:16-18). Fasting is not for the knowledge of others. Like all true prayer, fasting is primarily for the Lord.

Jesus was at a very important point when He fasted; He was about to begin His public ministry. When Moses fasted, He was on Mount Sinai for the second receiving of the Ten Commandments. In both cases the fasting provided assistance for prayer at very important junctures for the human race.[4]

The value of fasting lies in the concentration of our will on God.

࿐

Answer in your own words: How is fasting beneficial?

_____

_____

_____

What Is the Purpose of Prayerwalking?

Prayerwalking is a fast-growing movement practiced by thousands of believers. Prayerwalking is simply what it says—praying while you walk. It is praying with open eyes and an open heart while walking through a particular area, asking God to do a special work in that place.

Prayerwalking can be done anywhere Christians sense that God is leading them to pray. It can be as simple as praying for the people you meet and the homes you pass as you take a morning walk. A church or a mission group might enlist believers to walk through a neighborhood and pray for the people whose homes they pass. The strategy can be used to support a Vacation Bible School, a high school, or a revival meeting. It might take the form of walking through the preschool department at church, praying for children and workers, or it might be practiced while walking through a megacity in Asia, praying for the teeming throngs that crowd the streets and sidewalks.

One church has prayerwalking every Saturday evening at 6:00 p.m. As church members walk around the sanctuary, they pause and sit in every empty seat and pray a brief prayer for whoever may sit in that seat the next morning. When the pastor stands to preach on Sunday morning, he knows that every person present was prayed for the night before.

Another church conducted a prayerwalk around the church building at selected times for several weeks. As the pastor led church members around the building, he shared portions of the church's history, recounting God's blessings on the congregation, as well as trials the church had faced. Then the group spent time in prayer. The pastor said this strategy helped members move beyond painful memories and anticipate great things from God in the present and the future.

When you pray onsite, God seems to bring people and needs more sharply into focus.

Of course, you can pray for needs in your church or neighborhood and for needs in distant lands without leaving your home. But when you pray onsite, God seems to bring people and needs more sharply into focus. Prayerwalking is good not only for the recipients of the prayers but also for the prayerwalkers. It helps you become more sensitive to material, social, and spiritual needs around you and see those needs through God's eyes.

86

God has especially blessed prayerwalking in the work of missions around the world. Minette Drumwright, who served for a number of years as the director of the Office of International Prayer Strategy for the International Mission Board, organized the first planned prayer journey sponsored by the board. She writes:

> Prayerwalking covers the gamut of life. For example, I have prayerwalked university campuses in our country and on other continents, as well as hospitals, mosques, palaces, and parliament buildings. I have gone with prayerwalkers to areas where churches needed to be planted and covered the neighborhoods with intercession. I have met with prayerwalkers in elevated places high above a city. ... We pray for God to prepare the spiritual soil of the city for the gospel. We intercede for the people, praying they will be open and receptive to the transforming love of Jesus, asking the Holy Spirit to bring revival and spiritual awakening. I have driven through many high-crime areas, prayerfully asking the Father for the salvation of lives and for the transformation of troubled neighborhoods.[5]

Answer in your own words: What is the purpose of prayerwalking?

Does God Always Answer Prayer?

Not all prayers in the Bible were answered—at least not always with a yes. No, of course, is a legitimate answer. Most of the prayers in Scripture that received a no answer violate principles of prayer in significant ways. An examination of these examples reveals the patterns and ways God works through prayer.

Moses. As the Israelites once more rebelled in the wilderness, Moses petulantly asked to die (see Num. 11:11-15). Moses used 13 personal pronouns in this prayer, indicating that his eyes were off God and on himself. True prayer exalts God.

True prayer exalts God.

In Deuteronomy 3:23-29 Moses indicated that he had prayed to enter the promised land but that God would not permit this. In unbelief Moses had angrily struck the rock twice at Kadesh in disobedience to God's command to speak to the rock (see Num. 20:8-12). However, later God mercifully allowed Moses to survey the new land from the heights of Mount Nebo (see Deut. 32:48-52). Some sin is irreversible. We ourselves establish consequences for our actions that God will not suspend.

Saul. King Saul's inquiry of the Lord about the Philistines camped at Shunem was not answered (see 1 Sam. 28:6). A long record of sin against David, against the nation, and against God had separated him from God. Isaiah would later write that the Lord's ear was not dull so that it could not hear, "but your iniquities have made a separation between you and your God" (Isa. 59:2). Interestingly enough, two chapters after Saul's inquiry, David's inquiry about pursuing the Amalekites was answered (see 1 Sam. 30:8). This occurred in a time of great personal distress, when David had "strengthened himself in the Lord" (1 Sam. 30:6).

David. David's prayer for his son by Bathsheba to live was not answered (see 2 Sam. 12:15-20). David was praying for something about which God had already spoken. Nathan had warned him about his sin: " 'Because by this deed you have given occasion to the enemies of the Lord to blaspheme, the child also that is born to you shall surely die' " (2 Sam. 12:14). This child was the fruit of lust. An answer to David's prayer would have become a continual reminder of his sin.

Elijah. Elijah's prayer to die (see 1 Kings 19:4) is one of the strangest of the Bible prayers—not strange because God refused to answer but strange that the faith of Elijah could be so shattered after his great victory at Carmel. God still had use for Elijah, and Elijah simply stepped out of God's will in this prayer.

Salome, James, and John. Their prayer that the two sit at the right and left of Jesus was made from wrong motives (see Matt. 20:20-21). Jesus pointed out a factor that still holds true today in many of our prayers: " 'You do not know what you are asking for' " (v. 22).

James and John also mistakenly asked that fire from heaven consume the Samaritan village that refused to receive Christ (see Luke 9:51-56). This seemingly normal reaction represents the mind of humanity, not the mind of Christ.

> *"A child of God ought to expect answers to prayer. God means every prayer to have an answer. Not a single real prayer can fail of its effect in heaven."*[6]
> *—An unknown Christian*

Examples from Jesus' parables and teachings. Jesus referred twice in His parables and once in His teachings to types of unanswerable prayers. In the parable of the rich man and Lazarus, the rich man in hades asked that his tongue be cooled and his brothers warned (see Luke 16:19-31). This prayer was too late, and it involved nothing that all true prayer in the Bible is—it involved no worship of God (see Ps. 141:2), and it exhibited no fellowship, no commonality with God. Another of Jesus' parables pictures a self-exalting Pharisee boasting of his righteousness (see Luke 18:9-14). This is bragging, not praying. Again, it did not grow from fellowship with God. In a similar vein, Jesus pointed out that the street corner prayer of the hypocrites was not prayer (see Matt. 6:5). It was unanswerable. His conclusion is rather chilling: " 'Truly I say to you, they have their reward in full.' "

All prayers are not answered with a yes, in part because so many of them are counter to the nature of God's laws and to the mind of Christ. In addition, some "prayer" is not really prayer. James 5:17 has a curious expression in the Greek; speaking of Elijah, James wrote, "In prayer he prayed," which some translations render, "he prayed earnestly" (NASB). Halfheartedness and insincerity cannot characterize true prayer.

Job. Not all unanswered prayer is a result of failure in our prayers. Sometimes unanswered prayer may derive from a test God is imposing. Job's prayers did not involve sin, and the test came, not because he was in sin but because he was righteous. Tests are intended to prove both God's keeping power and our progress in His character.

Job's prayer to die (see Job 6:8-9) was made in ignorance of the heavenly council in Job 1, which was to be one of the great proofs of all time of the profound work that God can do in a person's life. Many of our prayers are in ignorance. We simply do not always know what is best, and we can only pray as best we know how. Abraham's prayer in ignorance (see Gen. 18:23-32) is beautiful proof that it is all right to pray in ignorance, outside the specific will of God, if we are praying within the character of God.

There is no record of sin in any of Job's prayers. It is interesting that three of the most righteous men in the Bible—Moses, Elijah, and Job—all mistakenly prayed to die. It is also interesting that they received great blessings from the Lord following their mistaken prayers.

"May my prayer be counted as incense before Thee; The lifting up of my hands as the evening offering" (Ps. 141:2).

We must be very careful about assuming that God is testing us or others when prayers are not answered. God deals with each of His children in the loving way that is best for their individual needs. The best we can do is to pray in trust and confidence. We can often learn valuable lessons in trust and patience in times of difficulty and testing. Trials are not necessarily sent by God, but He can always use them to draw us closer to Him. Such times of difficulty often prepare us for God's best that is still awaiting us.

Answer in your own words: Does God always answer prayer?

_____

_____

_____

_____

What If Your Prayers Are Not Answered?

"When the answer to our prayer does not come at once, we should combine quiet patience and joyful confidence in our persevering prayer."
—Andrew Murray
(1828–1917),
Scottish preacher and writer who pastored in South Africa

If our prayers are not answered, we have two choices: desist or persist. Paul prayed three times that his "thorn in the flesh" would be removed (see 2 Cor. 12:7-8). For the sake of the kingdom, pride on the part of this great church planter would have been disastrous. To check that pride, the Lord denied Paul his request, saying, " 'My grace is sufficient for you, for power is perfected in weakness' " (2 Cor. 12:9). Paul desisted from praying this prayer after that, preferring to boast about his weaknesses in order to have the power of the indwelling Christ.

When Daniel prayed in mourning for three weeks, the angel who came to encourage him told him, " 'Do not be afraid, Daniel, for from the first day that you set your heart on understanding this and on humbling yourself before your God, your words were heard, and I have come in response to your words' " (Dan. 10:12). The angel told him that he had been detained by a struggle with the "prince of the kingdom of Persia" (v. 13), but Michael had secured his release to come in answer to Daniel's prayer. At that point Daniel had been fasting and praying for three weeks. He persisted, and the result was a mighty and terrifying vision.

These two mighty men of God were so in tune with God that they knew when to persist and when to desist. That is what frightens us today. Few of us approach the keen spiritual sensitivity of a Paul or a Daniel. Nevertheless, the biblical record provides an example for us, and the potential of that kind of spiritual awareness is as great today as it was in the past.

We must also approach prayer with a willingness to accept God's actions with humility, regardless of our personal preferences. No doubt Zacharias and Elizabeth had long ago accepted a verdict of no when they prayed for a child. After a long delay Gabriel assured Zacharias, " 'Do not be afraid, Zacharias, for your petition has been heard' " (Luke 1:13). The couple had remained God's choice, even in their old age, and had not disqualified themselves with bitter resentment: "They were both righteous in the sight of God" (Luke 1:6). Their example is a live option for believers today who have not lost faith when answers seem long delayed.

Sometimes God Himself delays, as in the case of Zacharias; sometimes He allows evil forces to delay, as in Daniel's situation; sometimes the answer is no, as in the case of Paul. The qualities that are most likely to suffer in our character today during a delay are faith, patience, endurance, joy, and humble acceptance. We must guard against this loss, realizing that even delays can work out for our good.

We must approach prayer with a willingness to accept God's actions with humility, regardless of our personal preferences.

<(◦✿◦)>

Answer in your own words: What if your prayers are not answered?

_____

_____

_____

_____

_____

Does Prayer Change God's Mind?

After God rejected Saul as king over Israel, Saul pleaded with Samuel to come with him so that he could worship the Lord once again. Samuel refused, for God's verdict was final. He told Saul, " 'The Glory of Israel will not lie or change His mind; for He is not a man that He should change His mind' " (1 Sam. 15:29). Malachi quotes God as saying, " 'I, the Lord, do not change; therefore you, O sons of Jacob, are not consumed' " (Mal. 3:6). The New Testament presents the same picture: God is the "Father of lights, with whom there is no variation, or shifting shadow" (Jas. 1:17).

The attributes, purposes, and mind of God do not change.

We are often slow to discover the mind of God. God may have a specific end in view, with several possible routes toward that end. These various roads mean that the means of achieving God's end may be dynamic rather than static. God may now alter this or that road, may put up roadblocks, may redirect us in such a way that we who cannot see the end think that He seems to be changing. Our attention is on the road—and there are road rules—but God's attention is on the end. The attributes, purposes, and mind of God do not change, and we must be careful not to read into varying circumstances a purpose of God that would attribute change to Him.

Answer in your own words: Does prayer change God's mind?

_____

_____

_____

_____

When Is it Right to Pray for a Miracle?

Miracles in the Bible usually occurred in moments of desperation (as when Moses and the Israelites were blocked at the Red Sea) or when all other hope of help had been exhausted (like the various sick, lame, blind, and dumb who needed miracles of healing when they encountered Christ). Exceptions are the miracles surrounding Christ's death and resurrection, which are in a class by themselves. These served purposes different from the other biblical miracles.

The miracles in the Bible had certain factors in common:

1. They brought glory to God rather than human beings.
2. Sometimes they validated God's claims or identity.
3. They significantly advanced the divine work.
4. Capricious or whimsical motives are totally absent. Each biblical miracle exhibits an element of grandeur and awesome dignity, and each reflects a certain elegance (for lack of a better word) in its execution. This is easily demonstrable in Christ's miracles.

These same factors should exist today when we may expect a miracle. God may bring them together in our experience, and if He does, we can be sure He will enable us to recognize them and to pray in faith that He finish what He obviously started.

Miracles in the Bible brought glory to God rather than human beings.

Answer in your own words: When is it right to pray for a miracle?

_____

_____

_____

_____

_____

Does God Hear One Person More than Another?

A man once approached me to pray for a situation in such a way that it became apparent that he was asking me to pray because he felt I might have more influence with God than he; maybe I could get God to do what he could not persuade Him to do. The Bible nowhere substantiates such a notion. This was the way Saul wanted to use Samuel (see 1 Sam. 15:24-25).

It is true, of course, that God can be pleased and displeased with us. He seeks spiritual worshipers; He

Favors those who fear Him,
Those who wait for His lovingkindness" (Ps. 147:11).

There is joy in heaven over one sinner who repents (see Luke 15:7). We are told that the Lord takes pleasure in His people (see Ps. 149:4).

Individuals can please God. He asked Satan, " 'Have you considered My servant Job? For there is no one like him on the earth, a blameless and upright man, fearing God and turning away from evil' " (Job 1:8). Enoch was "pleasing to God" (Heb. 11:5). The angel called Daniel a "man of high esteem" (Dan. 10:11,19). Jesus loved Martha, Mary, and Lazarus (John 11:5), and John calls himself the "disciple whom Jesus loved" (John 20:2). These examples could be multiplied; the point is that a human being can become pleasing to the Lord, a joy to Him.

Although the Bible indicates that these beloved of the Lord received unusual answers to prayer, their answers did not indicate favoritism. Rather, these persons were obedient to the principles required by God and gave themselves with unstinting devotion to Him. They were not a favorite by arbitrary choice but were indeed favored because of the position they chose.

It is also evident that experienced prayer warriors can see factors, pray more intelligently, and weigh spiritual evidence in a way that prayerless people cannot. Many times I request prayer of certain people, not because I think they have influence with God but because I know they will pray.

When God's people become willing to exercise their privileges and prerogatives in prayer, great and mighty things will happen. His name will be glorified, and the world will become convinced that Jesus is indeed the Christ.

Dwight L. Moody's biography relates an experience Moody had with a prayer warrior that marked a turning point in the evangelist's career. In 1872 Moody went to England for a short trip, not intending to preach but to learn from the English Bible students there. However, while there Moody agreed to preach for Mr. Lessey, the pastor of a church in London.

Experienced prayer warriors can see factors, pray more intelligently, and weigh spiritual evidence in a way that prayerless people cannot.

94

The morning service seemed very dead and cold. The people did not show much interest, and he felt that it had been a morning lost. But at the next service, which was at half-past six in the evening, it seemed, while he was preaching, as if the very atmosphere was charged with the Spirit of God. There came a hush upon all the people, and a quick response to his words, though he had not been much in prayer that day, and could not understand it.

When he had finished preaching he asked all who would like to become Christians to rise, that he might pray for them. People rose all over the house until it seemed as if the whole audience was getting up. Mr. Moody said to himself, "These people don't understand me. They don't know what I mean when I ask them to rise." He had never seen such results before, and did not know what to make of it, so he put the test again. "Now," he said, "all of you who want to become Christians just step into the inquiry-room."

They went in, and crowded the room so that they had to take in extra chairs to seat them all. The minister was surprised, and so was Mr. Moody. Neither had expected such a blessing. They had not realized that God can save by hundreds and thousands as well as by ones and twos.

When Mr. Moody again asked those that really wanted to become Christians to rise, the whole audience got up. He did not even then know what to do, so he told all who were really in earnest to meet the pastor there the next night.[8]

Revival came, and Moody held meetings in the church for 10 days. Four hundred people made commitments to Christ. The evangelist wanted to know what made the difference between the cold morning service and the Spirit-filled evening service. He discovered that a bedfast woman, along with her sister, belonged to Mr. Lessey's church. The invalid was in perpetual pain, and her body was twisted and distorted by suffering. A woman of prayer, she earnestly prayed that God would send revival to her church. One day she read in a Christian paper about Dwight L. Moody's work in Chicago with poor children. She put the paper under her pillow and began praying that God would send the evangelist to her church.

"It is the heroes and heroines who are out of sight, and who labour in prayer, who make it possible for those who are in sight to do their work and win."[9]
—G. Campbell Morgan (1863–1945), pastor of Westminster Chapel, London

God hears the prayers of all His children.

On the Sunday Moody preached in her church, her sister came home and told her that a Mr. Moody from America had preached that morning. " 'I know what that means,' cried the sick woman. 'God has heard my prayers!' "[10] Moody said, "I found a bedridden girl praying that God would bring me to that Church. He had heard her, and brought me over four thousand miles of land and sea in answer to her request."[11]

God hears the prayers of all His children. And He answers!

ꙨꙨ

Answer in your own words: Does God hear one person more than another?

_____

_____

_____

_____

[1]Bertha Smith, chapel address, Southwestern Baptist Theological Seminary.

[2]Oswald Chambers, in *The One-Year Book of Personal Prayer* (Wheaton, IL: Tyndale House, 1991), September 7.

[3]Adapted from T. W. Hunt and Catherine Walker, *Disciple's Prayer Life* (Nashville: LifeWay Press, 1997), 188–89.

[4]Adapted from Hunt and Walker, *Disciple's Prayer Life,* 189-90.

[5]Minette Drumwright, *The Life That Prays: Reflections on Prayer as Strategy* (Birmingham: Woman's Missionary Union, 2001), 201.

[6]An unknown Christian, *The Kneeling Christian* (Grand Rapids: Zondervan, 1986), 87.

[7]Andrew Murray, *With Christ in the School of Prayer* (North Brunswick, NJ: Bridge-Logon Publishers, 1999), 125.

[8]William R. Moody, *The Life of Dwight L. Moody* (Murfreesboro, TN: Sword of the Lord Publishers, n.d.), 152–53.

[9]G. Campbell Morgan, *The Practice of Prayer* (Greenville, SC: Ambassador Productions, 1995), 110.

[10]Moody, *The Life of Dwight L. Moody,* 154.

[11]Morgan, *The Practice of Prayer,* 110.

Chapter 5
Overcoming Hindrances
to Effective Prayer

We know that Satan does not want Christians to pray and that he does everything he can to keep us from praying. The saying is true that Satan trembles when he sees the weakest saint on his knees. Immediately following the description of the armor of God that believers are to use to stand against the devil's schemes, Paul wrote: "Pray at all times in the Spirit, and with this in view, be on the alert with all perseverance and petition for all the saints" (Eph. 6:18).

"Pray at all times in the Spirit" (Eph. 6:18).

James tells us, "You do not have because you do not ask" (Jas. 4:2). How strange that such a warning should have been necessary after Jesus Himself gave so many injunctions to ask! Jesus told the woman at the well, " 'If you knew the gift of God, and who it is who says to you, "Give Me a drink," you would have asked Him, and He would have given you living water' " (John 4:10). This gentle offer was made to a woman who did not have the recorded promise that those who asked would receive. The numerous times Jesus used the word *ask* in His teaching prove the divine will to give. If progress in the Christian life depends on our prayers, if we are commanded to ask, if promises on a cosmic scale are made to those who ask, what would a waiting Father think if we refused to ask? The only possible conclusion would be that either we are not interested in spiritual progress or we intend to spurn the very Word of God.

Prayerlessness

A failure to pray is the first hindrance that a growing Christian must overcome. Some people may refuse to ask God in prayer because of a hypocritical piety that refuses to believe God's promises. The idolatrous king of Judah, Ahaz, when attacked by the northern kingdom of Syria, was assured by the prophet Isaiah that he need only ask for a sign from God. God would protect Judah, not for the sake of the faithless Ahaz but for the sake of God's people. Yet Ahaz assumed a superficially pious attitude: " 'I will not ask, nor will I test the Lord!' " (Isa. 7:12)—a cloak for his determination to rely on an alliance with Assyria rather than on Yahweh. Isaiah unmasked the hypocrisy: " 'Is it too slight a thing for you to try the patience of men, that you will try the patience of my God as well?' " (v. 13). It is indeed true that we are not to test God (see Deut. 6:16), but neither are we to spurn Him.

God's promises, like His commands, are not optional. The Ahaz account graphically illustrates the fact that a refusal to pray is an affront to a faithful God who has invited us to ask, seek, and knock. Prayerlessness is a statement to God that we do not believe that spiritual forces have the power to affect a world created by a spiritual Being. When we do not pray, we agree with Ahaz that security is found in the visible, in the forces of this world, even though we are repeatedly assured that all creation is under His dominion (see 1 Chron. 29:11-12; Pss. 97:1; 103:19).

" 'God is spirit' " (John 4:24), and it is He who ordained the way His world will function. Behind the functioning of this world is a spiritual hand that never errs, a spiritual mind that always operates. Pilate boasted of his own authority, but Jesus told him, " 'You would have no authority over Me, unless it had been given you from above' " (John 19:11). Many men of great public or personal stature were forced to acknowledge that the Lord Himself is God—for example, Nebuchadnezzar (see Dan. 4:1-3), Darius (see Dan. 6:25-27), and Saul of Tarsus (see Acts 9:1-16). It would be pointless to pray "for kings and all who are in authority" if we did not believe that such prayers would secure a "tranquil and quiet life in all godliness and dignity" (1 Tim. 2:2).

Only one kind of greatness is taught in the Bible—spiritual greatness. Prayerfulness characterized the lives of Enoch; Abraham; Moses; Hannah; Samuel; David; Hezekiah; Isaiah; Elijah; Elisha; Jeremiah; Daniel; Mary, the mother of Jesus; Peter; Paul; John; and, above all, Jesus, to mention only a very few. Can you imagine Daniel or Abraham or Jesus functioning apart from prayer? A life filled with the Spirit cannot be empty of prayer.

"Prayerlessness leaves the treasury of God's storehouse locked."[1]
—"Preacher" E. F. Hallock (1888–1978), pastor of First Baptist Church; Norman, Oklahoma

꧁ꕥ꧂

Listed below are common reasons many Christians do not spend much time praying. Check the two reasons that best describe your own lack of prayer at times. If these reasons do not apply to you, add your own problem in praying.

❑ Staying too busy
❑ Not taking time
❑ Doing what you want to do first and postponing communication with God
❑ Giving priority to other activities and things
❑ Putting God last
❑ Thinking prayer is not needed
❑ Believing you can take care of things on your own
❑ Not wanting to give God control of your life
❑ Other: _____

Now pray, asking God to help you obey each line of the verse in the margin.

Take time to be holy,
Speak oft with thy Lord;
Abide in Him always,
And feed on His Word.[2]

Prayerlessness is sin. When Israel sinned against the Lord by demanding a king, Samuel assured them in their fear, " 'As for me, far be it from me that I should sin against the Lord by ceasing to pray for you' " (1 Sam. 12:23). Paul was not guilty of this sin; he prayed for the churches "unceasingly" (Rom. 1:9), "always" (Phil. 1:4), and "night and day" (1 Thess. 3:10). He told Timothy, "I constantly remember you in my prayers night and day" (2 Tim. 1:3). Jesus' life was so prayerful that the disciples were moved to ask Him to teach them to pray (see Luke 11:1). His prayer for the disciples is a model of intercession (see John 17). Prayerlessness is never observed in any of the great men and women in the Bible.

There are many reasons Christians do not pray, all of them inexcusable.

The heart. Perhaps the main reason is the spiritual condition of the heart. If a person is cold and indifferent toward the things of God, prayer will hold little interest. Jesus made it clear that God is to be at the center of our heart: " 'Seek first His kingdom and His righteousness; and all these things shall be added to you' " (Matt. 6:33). Love for Him is preeminent (see Matt. 22:37). If we love Him, we long to spend time with Him.

"Why do you not pray? Have you no need to pray? Is there no good thing that God can give, and that you need? No earthly good for yourself or others? ... No spiritual good? Have you no sins to be forgiven? Have you no weakness to be helped, no temptations to struggle against? Have you no troubles? ... Why do you not pray?"[4]
—John A. Broadus (1827–95), a founder and the second president of Southern Baptist Theological Seminary

Time. Some people think they are too busy to take time to pray. In the 1800s Charles Spurgeon preached a sermon on hindrances to prayer. In that message Spurgeon said one reason Christians of that day did not pray was that they had too much to do and were too busy.[3] That was more than one hundred years ago—before automobiles and cell phones and fax machines and computers and television! The accelerated pace of life today makes busyness an even more frequent excuse.

Priorities. Sometimes a person's life is too cluttered and disorganized, without a personal schedule based on godly priorities. Some live a reactionary life, moving from task to task or from crisis to crisis. When Jesus was in the home of the three siblings of Bethany, Mary sat at His feet listening to what He said. "Martha was distracted with all her preparations" (Luke 10:40). Even among believers, there are too many modern-day Marthas and not enough Marys. Sometimes the good can crowd out the best (see v. 42).

Discipline. Some Christians have never developed the habit of prayer. They do not know the sweetness of daily communion with their Heavenly Father. A special place and a set time help cultivate the habit of prayer. The prophet Daniel cultivated the habit of prayer: "He continued kneeling on his knees three times a day, praying and giving thanks before his God" (Dan. 6:10). Jesus said, " 'When you pray, go into your inner room, and when you have shut your door, pray to your Father' " (Matt. 6:6). Jesus regularly took time to be alone with His Father: "When day came, He departed and went to a lonely place" (Luke 4:42).

The sin of prayerlessness is the most serious of all the hindrances to prayer. It balks at the beginning—and no progress is made if we start wrong. Prayerlessness is deadly.

꧁✤꧂

This is perhaps the most important activity in this book. How much time are you willing to spend each day in prayer? Stop and pray about this decision. Then check one of the following choices.
❑ **15 minutes**   ❑ **30 minutes**
❑ **45 minutes**   ❑ **1 hour**
❑ **Other:** _____

I commit to God that I will make every effort to spend _____ each day in prayer with Him.

Signed _____ Date_____

Pray, asking God to help you be faithful in keeping your commitment. Enlist someone to hold you accountable.

Wrong Motives

An attitude of selfishness resulting in wrong motives hinders effective prayer. James wrote, "You ask and do not receive, because you ask with wrong motives, so that you may spend it on your pleasures" (Jas. 4:3). When a person elevates his personal whims above those of others, the result is a separation, an isolation that loses sight of the larger goals of the body of Christ. Selfish desires pose one of the greatest dangers to personal growth and to church growth.

Paul showed us the legitimacy of prayer for self. His prayers for himself were for boldness to speak on behalf of the kingdom or for freedom to travel to a church that needed him. Hannah prayed for a son, but she gave him to the Lord. The self in these cases is deeply involved with others. The mind of Christ is to be concerned primarily with kingdom advance, God's will, and others' welfare. The self need not be selfish.

Selfishness poses a danger to the purposes God wants to accomplish. The psalmist wrote that the Israelites

Craved intensely in the wilderness,
And tempted God in the desert.
So He gave them their request,
But sent a wasting disease among them (Ps. 106:14-15).

In the rebellion at Taberah "the rabble who were among them had greedy desires" (Num. 11:4). The psalmist said that they

Put God to the test
By asking food according to their desire (Ps. 78:18).

The provision of manna by Yahweh did not satisfy them. The

Selfishness poses a danger to the purposes God wants to accomplish.

101

psalmist went on to say that this represented both unbelief and distrust (see Ps. 78:22). A selfish person is always discontented.

The New Testament is even more specific. Speaking of this rebellion, Paul warned, "These things happened as examples for us, that we should not crave evil things, as they also craved" (1 Cor. 10:6). He wrote to the church at Rome, "Make no provision for the flesh in regard to its lusts" (Rom. 13:14). He spelled out the principle in Galatians 5:17: "The flesh sets its desire against the Spirit, and the Spirit against the flesh; for these are in opposition to one another, so that you may not do the things that you please." Opposing natures cannot mix, and we must never mix opposing motives.

If you have a dog, you know that your pet has certain needs, like food, water, and affection. You share those needs, but some of your needs are different from the dog's because your natures are different. Your pleasure in the music of Beethoven means nothing to the dog; it has no need in that area and no way of understanding your need. You can romp with the dog and run with it, but the two of you can never listen to music together; it has no equipment to understand that part of your nature. Although you share certain things, your dog can partake of nothing uniquely human.

My animal needs are important, but they function best when they remain subservient to my spiritual needs. The animal part of me can serve the spirit, but I am most sublimely human when the spiritual is in control and dominates my entire being. This is why fasting can be a spiritual exercise. The animal needs are legitimate and healthy; they are not, in themselves, sin. The lesser, the animal, is subject to the greater, the spirit.

"A natural man does not accept the things of the Spirit of God; for they are foolishness to him, and he cannot understand them, because they are spiritually appraised" (1 Cor. 2:14).

The spirit and the body are not in opposition, but when the flesh (not the body) becomes a principle, a control for the spirit, either through pride (see Col. 2:18) or through lusts or any other manifestation (see Gal. 5:19-21), we have lowered the standard of our high creation in Christ. Just as a dog cannot conceive or understand that which is peculiarly human, a natural human cannot understand that which is peculiarly spirit (see 1 Cor. 2:14). And as a human is higher than an animal, a spiritual person lives in a higher dimension and understanding than a natural person. Jesus put it most succinctly: " 'It is the Spirit who gives life; the flesh profits nothing' " (John 6:63).

This is not to say that everyday human needs are not important. The Father knows that we need the ordinary things of life, and He is concerned about providing them for us (see Matt. 6:32). The point is that we are to give priority to His kingdom as we trust Him to supply our needs (see Matt. 6:33).

Selfishness brings into our experience a danger so great that God knows He cannot coddle us with answers that are hostile to the very thing He is working to achieve in us. I would not give a murderer a knife to pamper one of his whims. God will not risk putting into our hands a hazard in order to satisfy an unhealthy desire. Requests offered from totally selfish and wrong motives cannot be granted.

Requests offered from totally selfish and wrong motives cannot be granted.

Material things are not wrong in themselves. However, it is possible for Christians to let material things push aside spiritual things, and a Christian's focus can be misplaced. Selfishness can take root and hinder prayer. Examine the following list and ask yourself:
• Are any of these areas too important in my life?
• Do I pray about these areas with a selfish motive?
• Do any of these areas hinder my service to God through my church?
• Do any of these areas hurt my witness for Christ?
• Do any of these areas harm my Christian influence in my community and workplace?
• Do any of these areas hinder my reaching out and helping others?

Check each area that represents a problem for you.

❑ career/work/school	❑ clothes
❑ house	❑ money/investments
❑ personal appearance	❑ travel
❑ television	❑ sports/recreation
❑ hobbies	❑ clubs/organizations
❑ eating/appetite/food	❑ collections
❑ cars	❑ social standing
❑ other: _____	

Ask God to help you keep material things in their proper place and give priority to spiritual things.

Lack of Faith

Faith is the basis of any genuine relationship. The more sensitive and dynamic a relationship is, the greater the faith that must enter into it. The writer of Hebrews stated, "Without faith it is impossible to please Him, for he who comes to God must believe that He is, and that He is a rewarder of those who seek Him" (Heb. 11:6). Failure to believe means that we think that God is a liar and that He is mocking us. No relationship is possible without faith.

Wavering is the opposite of God's character. He does not change. One secret of successful praying is to duplicate God's character. In the verses in the margin, James puts a special emphasis on the role of character in prayer. Stop and read those verses.

In the world you normally earn what you get. But in God's kingdom you get what you believe. After giving the figure of speech about faith moving mountains, Jesus said, " 'I say to you, all things for which you pray and ask, believe that you have received them, and they shall be granted you' " (Mark 11:24). The believing is the receiving, and without the believing there is no receiving.

"If any of you lacks wisdom, let him ask of God, who gives to all men generously and without reproach, and it will be given to him. But let him ask in faith without any doubting, for the one who doubts is like the surf of the sea driven and tossed by the wind. For let not that man expect that he will receive anything from the Lord, being a double-minded man, unstable in all his ways" (Jas. 1:5-8).

Faith is the cup we offer to God to fill, and it is a measuring cup. When the centurion demonstrated great faith, Jesus told him, " 'Let it be done to you as you have believed' " (Matt. 8:13). Apparently, the centurion's faith was equal to the situation, for His servant was healed "that very hour." Because the officer demonstrated such faith that he believed that Jesus could heal across distances, Jesus marveled, " 'Truly I say to you, I have not found such great faith with anyone in Israel' " (v. 10).

Jesus often measured the faith of those who came to Him. He asked two blind men seeking healing, " 'Do you believe that I am able to do this?' " When they answered yes, he told them, " 'Be it done to you according to your faith' " (Matt. 9:28-29). Their faith measured high, for their eyes were opened.

Two causes may underlie difficulty in believing.

A fear that God does not want to give. The repeated invitations to ask are proof of the divine intention. Jesus' words when He raised Lazarus demonstrated His desire that we believe. Standing before the tomb, He prayed: " 'Father, I thank Thee that Thou heardest Me. And I knew that Thou hearest Me always; but because of the people standing around I said it, that they may believe that Thou didst send Me' " (John 11:41-42). God's desire is that we may believe.

A fear that what we are asking is too great or too difficult. The irrationality of this fear is unmasked when we recognize that we are actually afraid that God cannot perform. God's word to Jeremiah was " 'Behold, I am the Lord, the God of all flesh; is anything too difficult for Me?' " (Jer. 32:27). The prophet knew the answer to God's question and had already expressed it: " ' "Ah Lord God! Behold, Thou hast made the heavens and the earth by Thy great power and by Thine outstretched arm! Nothing is too difficult for Thee" ' " (Jer. 32:17). At the foot of the mount of transfiguration, when the pleading father asked Jesus whether He could do anything for his demon-possessed son, Jesus exclaimed, " 'If You can! All things are possible to him who believes' " (Mark 9:23). God is the possessor of all riches; we never need wonder whether He can afford what we might ask. He is the author of all capabilities; we never need wonder whether He can produce.

> *God is the author of all capabilities; we never need wonder whether He can produce.*

⟪◖◌⟡◌◗⟫

In the next five paragraphs underline ideas for increasing your faith. Circle an action you will take.

Faith changes behavior. The Greek word for *receiving* and *taking* is the same. Jesus said that if we ask, we will receive; if we ask, we are to take. Paul's behavior grew from his prayer. From prison he wrote the Philippians, "I know that this shall turn out for my deliverance through your prayers and the provision of the Spirit of Jesus Christ" (Phil. 1:19). No worry, no apprehension pervades the rest of this letter; this is, in fact, the most joy-filled letter in the New Testament.

The work, after all, does not depend on our resources, talents, or training. It is Christ who is in us (see Gal. 2:20), who wants us to believe, through whom we have access to God (see Eph. 3:12). Romans 10:17, "Faith comes from hearing, and hearing by the word of Christ," is an extremely crucial verse in understanding how faith develops. Faith in Christ is our means of access to the throne of God. Paul said, "We have boldness and confident access through faith in him" (Eph. 3:12). He overcame every trial and every temptation and defeated even death itself. Death is the final and greatest threat any of us face—and yet Jesus conquered death. In doing so, He triumphed over all of the rulers of hell: "When He had disarmed the rulers and authorities, He made a public display of them, having triumphed over them through Him" (Col. 2:15). He defeated Satan's highest efforts. He triumphed over the most that hell could offer. He has done everything possible to help us believe. The greatest secret to faith is concentrating on Him and putting our attention on His message.

We are to hold on to our confidence in Christ. When we became Christians, we placed our faith in Christ. We had confidence in Him and in what He did for us on the cross. We believed that He could and would save us. The writer of Hebrews calls us to hold on to that same confidence steadfastly: "We have become partakers of Christ, if we hold fast the beginning of our assurance firm until the end" (Heb. 3:14). We are never to let it go.[5]

If we believe God, we can leave the case in His hands. Paul wrote that we are to "be anxious for nothing" (Phil. 4:6) and then assured us that God's peace would "guard your hearts and your minds in Christ Jesus" (v. 7). Faith frees us to do God's work without impediment from within.

The function of faith is not simply to get something done. Faith is the basis of our relationship with God. That relationship is significant truth—the truth of a divinely initiated relationship with a great Father, a caring Shepherd, and a gentle Master. We can put our confidence in our gracious Lord.

Not Abiding

Failure to maintain a vital relationship with God hinders prayer. Any relationship must be nurtured, and the most important relationship in life is especially sensitive. Jesus told the disciples, " 'If you abide in Me, and My words abide in you, ask whatever you wish, and it shall be done for you' " (John 15:7). Anyone can make a superficial claim of any cause; the world and the kingdom see many crusaders who are here today and gone tomorrow. Genuineness is proved by enduring in the beliefs we profess.

" 'If you abide in Me, and My words abide in you, ask whatever you wish, and it shall be done for you' " (John 15:7).

Paul wrote that God would "render to every man according to his deeds: to those who by perseverance in doing good seek for glory and honor and immortality, eternal life" (Rom. 2:6-7). Each of these words is cosmic in scope—*glory, honor, immortality, eternal life.* How long did it take for David to win glory or for Daniel to establish honor? Nothing temporary is seen in the work of Joseph, Samuel, Paul, or Jesus. Love "bears all things, believes all things, hopes all things, endures all things" (1 Cor. 13:7). Abiding is not accomplished in an afternoon's time. This is not to say that only the spiritually mature can pray effectively, nor does it advocate spiritual elitism. God hears the prayers of all His children. It is to say, however, that a continuing relationship with Christ enhances prayer.

A continuing relationship with Christ enhances prayer.

The word *walk* is an important word in the New Testament. It is a picture word, describing what it means to abide in Christ. It describes a Christian's continuing daily life. John revealed that this continuing process proves that we belong to Christ: "By this we know that we are in Him: the one who says he abides in Him ought himself to walk in the same manner as He walked" (1 John 2:5-6). Paul was fond of the word *walk;* he advised the Ephesians to walk in love, to walk as light, and to walk wisely (Eph. 5:2,8,15). If we are abiding in Christ, we cannot comfortably walk any other way.

God is more interested in a good root system than in the foliage of our lives. We tend to dress up the foliage, but God wants a healthy, extensive root system. He concluded the parable of the sower by observing that the seed in the good ground " 'are the ones who have heard the word in an honest and good heart, and hold it fast, and bear fruit with perseverance' " (Luke 8:15).

My family once lived for a while in Spain, where we were fascinated to observe the extensive farming of grapes. On many farms the grapes are not slender vines, as so often seen in America, but have thick trunks. We were astonished at the end of the harvest to see the Spaniards cutting down those treelike vines. But the next season their stumps began to grow shoots. Most surprising of all was to watch the workers prune the branches so thoroughly. Once we even saw a farmer placing rocks on the stumps to force the shoots to grow exactly as he wanted. It was evident that the root systems were undamaged. The plant's life depends only a little on its foliage but very much on its roots. To the Spanish farmers, foliage was secondary. It was fruit that was important, and the workers entered the process of getting that fruit by maintaining good roots and pruning the branches.

Why is abiding important? It is one aspect of endurance. It is proof of faithfulness. Only in abiding is importunity, or persistence, a real option. Abiding demonstrates a part of our character that is like God, whose "righteousness endures forever" (Ps. 111:3) and whose name is everlasting (see Ps. 135:13).

Abiding entails much time, much prayer, much attention to the biblical directives, and much cleaving to the Lord. For me, at least, it has involved a serious attempt to memorize much Scripture. Most encouraging is the fact that abiding requires no talent or training; it requires only perseverance.

⋘◦⟊◦⟩⟩

Following are components of abiding in Christ. As you read each, ask, *Does this characterize my life?* Then circle a number on the scale. 1 = very seldom in your life. 3 = sometimes present. 5 = often present in your life.

I maintain a vital relationship with God.	1	2	3	4	5
I pray each day.	1	2	3	4	5
I ask without doubt in my heart.	1	2	3	4	5
I recognize God's authority and power to answer.	1	2	3	4	5
I have confidence in God's purposes for my life.	1	2	3	4	5
I have confidence in God's care for me.	1	2	3	4	5
I read my Bible each day.	1	2	3	4	5
I believe that God speaks to me through His Word.	1	2	3	4	5
I claim the promises of God's Word.	1	2	3	4	5
My life is characterized by constancy.	1	2	3	4	5
I depend on the Holy Spirit to guide me.	1	2	3	4	5
I worship God with other believers in my church.	1	2	3	4	5
I reach out to others and minister in Jesus' name to persons in need.	1	2	3	4	5
I share with others about Jesus.	1	2	3	4	5
My life bears spiritual fruit.	1	2	3	4	5
Others can see Christ living in me.	1	2	3	4	5

Thank God for His presence and guidance in your life. Ask Him to help you where you need to grow stronger.

"Prayer is not some battering ram by which we gain entrance to God's treasury. It is a receptacle by which we receive that which He already longs to give to us."[6]
—Herschel H. Hobbs (1907–95), Baptist theologian; author; pastor of First Baptist Church; Oklahoma City, Oklahoma; and president of the Southern Baptist Convention, 1961–63

Rebellion and Sin

Scripture teaches that an attitude of rebellion in the heart or sin in the life hinders prayer. An ancient indictment of Israel has served as a solemn warning for all time. Read Isaiah 59:1-2 in the margin.

Peter wrote:

"The eyes of the Lord are upon the righteous,
And His ears attend to their prayer,
But the face of the Lord is against those who do evil" (1 Pet. 3:12).

Any and all sin hinders effective prayer. You get in your car and turn on the ignition, but nothing happens. You find that the battery cable is corroded, breaking the connection so that the current cannot get through. Sin is like that. It can corrode your life and break the connection with God. The foundation of authentic prayer is a right relationship with God. Solomon wrote:

The sacrifice of the wicked is an abomination to the Lord,
But the prayer of the upright is His delight.
The Lord is far from the wicked,
But He hears the prayer of the righteous (Prov. 15:8,29).

Any sin will annul the authority of our prayers, but the Bible specifically names several sins—besides the others discussed in this chapter—that immediately block our prayers.

Unconfessed sin hinders prayer. The psalmist wrote,

If I had cherished sin in my heart,
the Lord would not have listened (Ps. 66:18, NIV).

The word *cherish* is translated in the *King James Version* as *regarded*. This Hebrew word has various shades of meaning, including *to view, to look at.*[7] It carries the idea of *holding on to and not confessing*. We cannot hold on to sin and expect God to hear our prayers. God said:

"When you spread out your hands in prayer,
I will hide My eyes from you,
Yes, even though you multiply prayers,
I will not listen.

"Behold, the Lord's hand
   is not so short
That it cannot save;
Neither is His ear so dull
That it cannot hear.
But your iniquities have
   made a separation
   between you and
   your God,
And your sins have hidden
   His face from you,
   so that He does not
   hear" (Isa. 59:1-2).

Your hands are covered with blood.
Wash yourselves, make yourselves clean;
Remove the evil of your deeds from My sight.
Cease to do evil,
Learn to do good" (Isa. 1:15-17).

Confession and cleansing are required before your fellowship with God is restored and you can make the connection with Him in prayer. If you look into your heart and see sin, you must acknowledge that sin to God and ask His forgiveness. John wrote, "If we confess our sins, He is faithful and righteous to forgive us our sins and to cleanse us from all unrighteousness" (1 John 1:9).

Idolatry hinders prayer. Idolatry was a persistent barrier between ancient Israel and God. Ezekiel quoted God as saying: " 'Son of man, these men [elders of Israel] have set up their idols in their hearts, and have put right before their faces the stumbling block of their iniquity. Should I be consulted by them at all?' " (Ezek. 14:3). God will not be consulted by anyone who has elevated something in the heart above Himself. Note that the warning is not against idols on the altar—it is against idols in the heart. On another occasion Ezekiel had a vision in which he was lifted by the Spirit of God and carried to Jerusalem. There he saw not only God's glory but also abominable idols the people were worshiping. Then God said, " 'Son of man, do you see what they are doing, the great abominations which the house of Israel are committing here, that I should be far from My sanctuary? But yet you will see still greater abominations' " (Ezek. 8:6). The prophet was led by God to the entrance to the court, where he saw a hole in the wall. God commanded him to dig into the wall. The amazed prophet came to a doorway. Read in the margin what happened next.

The spiritual leaders of Israel were worshiping idols in their hearts. Those who had the awesome responsibility of leading the people to worship only the Lord God had themselves fallen into deep idolatry. The Israelites felt that they had kept the second commandment: " 'You shall not make for yourself an idol, or any likeness of what is in heaven above or on the earth beneath or in the water under the earth' " (Ex. 20:4). They kept physical idols out of their homes and off their altars but had idols in their hearts.

But idols are not limited to ancient Israel. America is a land of idols. An idol is anything we put in the place of God. It can be tele-

"He said unto me, 'Go in and see the wicked abominations that they are committing here.' So I entered and looked, and behold, every form of creeping things and beasts and detestable things, with all the idols of the house of Israel, were carved on the wall all around. And standing in front of them were seventy elders of the house of Israel, ... each man with his censer in his hand, and the fragrance of the cloud of incense rising. Then He said to me, 'Son of man, do you see what the elders of the house of Israel are committing in the dark, each man in the room of his carved images? For they say, "The Lord does not see us; the Lord has forsaken the land" ' " (Ezek. 8:9-12).

vision or money, a hobby or a career. It can be something sinful in itself (see Col. 3:5). We can even put noble and worthy things, though good in themselves, above God.

Many Americans have borrowed a practice from the ancient Samaritans. Following the conquest of the northern kingdom Israel in 721 B.C., the Assyrians took many people from their homeland into captivity. As was their custom, the Assyrians then brought in colonists from various regions to repopulate the land of Israel. These people intermarried with the Israelites who were left in Israel, giving rise to the Samaritan race. The resulting religious practice was an odd mixture of paganism and the worship of God: "They worshiped the Lord, but they also served their own gods" (2 Kings 17:33, NIV). Similarly, many people today give lip service to God, at the same time serving their own gods.

God is jealous for our hearts. He does not tolerate any competition for our loyalty, so we must not elevate anything above Himself. Anything we love more than God is an idol, and it hinders prayer. If our prayers are to be effective, every idol must be renounced. There must be nothing between us and God.

Neglect of the Bible hinders prayer. Reading the Bible is a vital part of prayer. When we read the Bible, God speaks to us. Without regular study of God's Word, our prayers become shallow and ineffective (see Prov. 28:9). After the death of Moses, God said to Joshua: " 'This Book of the Law shall not depart from your mouth, but you shall meditate on it day and night, so that you may be careful to do according to all that is written in it' " (Josh. 1:8). Several generations later, the psalmist opened the Hebrew songbook by declaring that a righteous person delights in the law of the Lord and meditates on it day and night (see Ps. 1:2).

Jesus emphasized the relationship between staying in God's Word and receiving answers to prayer: " 'If you abide in Me and My words abide in you, ask whatever you wish, and it shall be done for you' " (John 15:7). If we neglect the Bible, we cannot expect God to hear and answer our prayers.

Prayer and Scripture are inseparably linked. At least four qualities of Scripture make it valuable for prayer.

1. The Bible provides preparation for prayer. Reading the Bible helps us focus our thoughts on God's character and nature in relationship to His people, thus preparing our minds for prayer.
2. Scripture provides guidance. It is a trustworthy guide for living

"Consider the members of your earthly body as dead to immorality, impurity, passion, evil desire, and greed, which amounts to idolatry" (Col. 3:5).

"Thy word is a lamp to my feet, And a light to my path" (Ps. 119:105).

(see Ps. 119:105). Even as we pray and ask God for guidance, we find it in His Word.

3. Scripture provides God's wisdom. God's wisdom is not hidden; any of us can understand as much as is necessary for our prayers. Again, as we pray for wisdom, we find it in His Word.

4. Scripture provides subjects for prayer. We find in the Bible many things we can ask for ourselves and for others. For example, Paul prayed for the Ephesians, "I pray that out of His glorious riches He may strengthen you with power through his Spirit in your inner being, so that Christ may dwell in your hearts through faith" (Eph. 3:16-17, NIV). We might read this Scripture and then pray that our inner being be made stronger through the Holy Spirit and that Christ dwell more completely in our hearts.

Jesus is our supreme example in using Scripture in prayer and in every area of life. The Scriptures were constantly in Jesus' mind, affecting the way He spoke and prayed. Because He had memorized Scripture, it was available to Him at any time. Jesus prepared His mind and heart with Scripture to resist temptation and taught us to pray, " 'Do not lead us into temptation, but deliver us from evil' " (Matt. 6:13). Jesus also used the words of Scripture in some of His prayers. Two prayers He uttered on the cross were direct quotations of Scripture. His cry " 'My God, My God, why hast Thou forsaken Me?' " (Matt. 27:46) is the beginning of the great messianic psalm on crucifixion, Psalm 22. His final prayer, " 'Father, into Thy hands I commit My spirit' " (Luke 23:46), quoted Psalm 31:5. Jesus' mind was saturated with Scripture. In the extremities of life He had access to inspired words to express prayers of an intensity we cannot imagine. Our prayer lives will be richer and more pleasing to God when refined by the truths of His Word.

Hypocrisy hinders prayer. The sin of hypocrisy in prayer reaps its own reward, but it reaps nothing from the Lord. Jesus cautioned: " 'When you pray, you are not to be as the hypocrites; for they love to stand and pray in the synagogues and on the street corners, in order to be seen by men. Truly I say to you, they have their reward in full' " (Matt. 6:5). Pretense in prayer is speaking to human beings rather than to God. Jesus cautioned again, " 'Beware of the scribes who like to walk around in long robes, and like respectful greetings in the market places, and chief seats in the synagogues, and places of honor at banquets, who devour widows' houses, and for appearance's sake offer long prayers; these will receive greater condemnation' " (Mark 12:38-40). When we pray for the sake of appearance, we get what appearance can give. Fleshly prayer bears no spiritual fruit.

Self-righteousness hinders prayer. Closely related to hypocrisy, an attitude of self-righteousness negates our prayers. Some people think that because of who they are or what they do, God must pay special attention to their prayers. When we have this attitude, we cannot connect with God. Jesus issued this warning to those who are self-righteous and look down on others. Read His parable in the margin.

God is with the humble. Isaiah wrote,

Thus says the high and exalted One
Who lives forever, whose name is Holy,
"I dwell on a high and holy place,
And also with the contrite and lowly of spirit" (Isa. 57:15).

Because God dwells with the humble, they are in constant contact with Him. They have His attention (see Ps. 138:6). Humility is required to truly exalt God and others above self.

Anger hinders prayer. Paul warned against anger in prayer: "I want the men in every place to pray, lifting up holy hands, without wrath or dissension" (1 Tim. 2:8). Anger opposes God's character. It is true that anger is an attribute of God, but His anger is different from the anger of people. God never "gets mad." His anger is a permanent, unchanging attribute of His holy nature. He is eternally angry at sin, unrighteousness, and injustice—attributes that are opposite His character. His anger never smolders or flares; it is, like His purity, transcendent, other, holy. On the other hand, "the anger of man does not achieve the righteousness of God" (Jas. 1:20). Human wrath is unholy. It is usually sudden and vindictive. When people become angry, they often lose control or hold grudges for a long time. Such anger hinders our prayers.

Broken relationships hinder prayer. Being in conflict with others keeps us from being effective in prayer. Jesus strongly warned against coming to God with a bitter heart that maintains a broken relationship: " 'If therefore you are presenting your offering at the altar, and there remember that your brother has something against you, leave your offering there before the altar, and go your way; first be reconciled to your brother, and then come and present your offering' " (Matt. 5:23-24). This warning applies primarily to

" 'Two men went up into the temple to pray, one a Pharisee, and the other a tax-gatherer. The Pharisee stood and was praying thus to himself, "God, I thank Thee that I am not like other people: swindlers, unjust, adulterers, or even like this tax-gatherer. I fast twice a week; I pay tithes of all that I get." But the tax-gatherer, standing some distance away, was even unwilling to lift up his eyes to heaven, but was beating his breast, saying, "God, be merciful to me, the sinner!" I tell you, this man went down to his house justified rather than the other; for everyone who exalts himself shall be humbled, but he who humbles himself shall be exalted' " (Luke 18:10-14).

our need of forgiveness from others. Our offenses usually grow from expressions of selfishness—the antithesis of our character as children of God. Seeking forgiveness is an expression of humility, which is of great value in the kingdom.

The close relationship of marriage has the potential of great power in prayer. But close relationships are sensitive, and it is dangerous to allow a fractured relationship to hinder a potentially powerful relationship with the Lord. Peter gave instructions to both the wife and the husband about respect and sensitivity in the marriage relationship. He warned that prayers could be hindered by a breakdown in this area (see 1 Pet. 3:7).

Outer conflict is a sign of inner conflict, and conflict is foreign to the nature of God's kingdom. We are told, "If possible, so far as it depends on you, be at peace with all men" (Rom. 12:18). This suggests that at times one person or party may be innocent and yet have to deal with a second party who is unwilling to make peace. Our main responsibility is for the part that depends on us. Again Paul exhorted, "Let us pursue the things which make for peace and the building up of one another" (Rom. 14:19). That we can do. The importance of this pursuit is revealed by the number of times it is enjoined in Scripture (see Ps. 34:14; 1 Tim. 2:22; Heb. 12:14). The life of Christ in the individual and in the larger body, the church, should be a whole life, a unified life, integrated and without conflict. Splintering what God unites interferes with the other work of God—His work through our prayers.

An unforgiving spirit hinders prayer. Failure to forgive others, certainly indicative of a broken relationship, interferes with our prayers. Jesus taught more on this subject than on any other hindering sin. Take a moment to read His words in the margin.

Peter wanted to find out exactly how far a forgiving spirit should go. The rabbis taught people to forgive three times,[8] so Peter went far beyond their teaching. Surely seven times would be more than enough. But Jesus replied, " 'I tell you, not seven times, but seventy-seven times' " (Matt. 18:22, NIV). We are not to keep score. There is no limit to God's forgiveness; neither should there be a limit to ours. Then Jesus told the parable of the unforgiving servant to illustrate the seriousness of forgiving others (see Matt. 18:23-35).

A person may object, "But you don't know what so-and-so did to me!" Even so, we know what we did to God. Jesus' sacrifice of Himself for our sins was so costly that He dearly values a forgiv-

" 'If you forgive men for their transgressions, your heavenly Father will also forgive you. But if you do not forgive men, then your Father will not forgive your transgressions' " (Matt. 6:14-15).

" 'Whenever you stand praying, forgive, if you have anything against anyone; so that your Father also who is in heaven may forgive you your transgressions' " (Mark 11:25).

ing spirit. Forgiveness duplicates His character in you. It is Godlike to forgive. We pay a very high penalty when we refuse to be like Him. If we demonstrate an unforgiving spirit, God does not forgive us, and our prayers are hindered.

Indifference to the needs of the weak and helpless hinders prayer. Jesus has a special place in His heart for persons on the backside of society—the prisoners, the brokenhearted, the poor and trampled down, the weak and helpless, the sick and suffering, the cold and hungry. He began His ministry by declaring that He had come to minister to them (see Luke 4:17-18). He later taught that in the final judgment the way we treat these people will reveal our character (see Matt. 25:31-46). The early church took seriously the matter of caring for those in need: "This is pure and undefiled religion in the sight of our God and Father, to visit orphans and widows in their distress, and to keep oneself unstained by the world" (Jas. 1:27).

From the unborn to the very old—and every age group in between—Christians today must reach out and minister to the needy in Christ's love. The sin of abortion hangs like a dark cloud over America. When we as a nation turn our backs on the unborn, our prayers are hindered. Indifference to the needs of the weak and helpless is sin. Shutting our ears against need is unlike God. In contrast, an open-hearted generosity is like God and wins His heart. God does not hear the prayer of anyone who mistreats the needy and innocent or denies help to them.

Withholding tithes and offerings hinders prayer. Giving tithes and offerings is a part of our total stewardship of life. It acknowledges God's ownership of everything and expresses our thanksgiving for His many blessings. God is displeased when we fail to return a token of what He has blessed us with. About one hundred years after the Jews had returned to their land after their exile, they had grown lax in many areas of worship. One area was stewardship. God spoke to the people: " 'Will a man rob God? Yet you are robbing Me! But you say, "How have we robbed Thee?" In tithes and offerings. You are cursed with a curse, for you are robbing Me, the whole nation of you! Bring the whole tithe into the storehouse, so that there may be food in My house, and test Me now in this,' says the Lord of hosts, 'if I will not open for you the windows of heaven, and pour out for you a blessing until it overflows' " (Mal. 3:8-10). We cannot expect God to hear our prayers and pour out His blessings on us if we withhold our tithes and offerings.

"He who shuts his ear to the cry of the poor, Will also cry himself and not be answered" (Prov. 21:13).

Prayerfully study the self-evaluation and mark each continuum to indicate where you believe you are.

Hold on to sin	Regularly confess sin
Put other things before God	Always put God first
Sporadic Bible study	Daily Bible study
More concerned about what others think	More concerned about what God thinks
Proud, rely on self	Humble, depend on God
Prone to anger, hot temper	Calm under pressure
Tendency toward conflict	Peaceable, free from strife
Hold grudges, resentment	Forgive others
Indifferent to others	Generous toward others
Stingy toward God	Cheerfully give to God

"Be gracious to me, O God, according to Thy lovingkindness; According to the greatness of Thy compassion blot out my transgressions. Wash me thoroughly from my iniquity, And cleanse me from my sin. Create in me a clean heart, O God, And renew a steadfast spirit within me" *(Ps. 51:1-2,10).*

Pray about the areas you marked on the left of the scales. Use words from Psalm 51, in the margin, to confess your sin and to ask for forgiveness.

Lack of Persistence

Jesus' teachings reveal that He valued persistence, or importunity, most highly (see chap. 2, especially on Luke 11:5-13; 18:1-8). God works in process, always perfect in its timing but sometimes discouraging to us if our faith is not strong. Mark 4:26-29 describes a seed's imperceptible growth to its ultimate harvest and assumes the farmer's patience as a part of the process.

Importunity accomplishes much in our growth. It toughens faith. It establishes the reality of abiding and endurance. It proves earnestness, humility, obedience, and patience. We are to be slow to anger but also slow to give up.

Even from a human standpoint it is easy to see the reasonableness and the need for persistence in prayer. Often someone pleads with me, "Please don't stop praying for me." When the Philistines mustered against Israel at Mizpah, the Israelites begged Samuel, " 'Do not cease to cry to the Lord our God for us, that He may save us from the hand of the Philistines' " (1 Sam. 7:8). Paul asked the Ephesian church to "be on the alert with all perseverance and petition for all the saints, and pray on my behalf" (Eph. 6:18-19). It encourages anyone to know that he or she is being prayed for—and that may be one reason persistence is pleasing to God.

It encourages anyone to know that he or she is being prayed for—and that may be one reason persistence is pleasing to God.

Listed below are the hindrances to prayer that you have studied. Think about each item and ask yourself, *Does this characterize my life?* Then circle a number on the scale for each item. 1 = very seldom in your life. 3 = sometimes present. 5 = often present in your life.

Prayerlessness	1	2	3	4	5
Wrong motives	1	2	3	4	5
Lack of faith	1	2	3	4	5
Not abiding	1	2	3	4	5
Rebellion and sin	1	2	3	4	5
Lack of persistence	1	2	3	4	5

What are you willing to do to eliminate the hindrances to prayer in your life? Ask God for forgiveness and strength to help you turn away from them.

*Nothing between my soul
and the Saviour,
So that His blessed face
may be seen;
Nothing preventing
the least of His favor,
Keep the way clear!
Let nothing between.*

*Nothing between
like worldly pleasure;
Habits of life,
though harmless they seem,
Must not my heart
from Him ever sever—
He is my all,
there's nothing between.*

*Nothing between,
like pride or like station;
Self or friends
shall not intervene;
Though it may cost me
much tribulation,
I am resolved,
there's nothing between.*[9]

This chapter named particular hindrances to prayer, but remember that any sin blocks the action of prayer, and any hindrance is from our side. In sin we are unlike God, and we cannot understand Him. In sin we are blinded and do not know what to ask for. In sin we act apart from His nature, and this brings barriers from God on our paths, which, if we are sensitive, could suggest better ways. Not receiving answers, many people become bitter and even more estranged from God. Sin begets sin (see Jas. 3:16) and confuses our prayer life.

Sometimes a part of the delay we experience in prayer is the responsibility of divine wisdom. God cannot perpetuate error or unholiness. If He did that, the answer to prayer would itself be sin, and God cannot sin. He will not allow blindness to worsen with an improper answer, and He will not allow character to soften with too soon an answer. If we sin, He will lovingly bring us back to a point where we can begin learning again of His grand and perfect plan for our lives. That plan will be finished, and the body of Christ will be established through our prayers. That is His method.

---

[1] E. F. Hallock, *Always in Prayer* (Nashville: Broadman Press, 1966), 39.

[2] William D. Longstaff, "Take Time to Be Holy," in *The Baptist Hymnal* (Nashville: Convention Press, 1991), 446.

[3] C. H. Spurgeon, *Prayer* (Greenville, SC: Emerald House, 1998), 131.

[4] John A Broadus, *Sermons and Addresses* (Baltimore: H. M. Wharton, 1888), 68.

[5] Adapted from T. W. Hunt and Catherine Walker, *Disciple's Prayer Life* (Nashville: LifeWay Press, 1997), 153–54.

[6] Herschel H. Hobbs, *An Exposition of the Gospel of Matthew* (Grand Rapids: Baker Book House, 1965), 73.

[7] Spiros Zodhiates, ed., *Hebrew-Greek Key Study Bible* (Chattanooga: AMG Publishers, 1984), 1658.

[8] Charles Caldwell Ryrie, *Ryrie Study Bible* (Chicago: Moody Press, 1986), 1344.

[9] C. A. Tindley, "Nothing Between," in *Soul-Stirring Songs and Hymns* (Murfreesboro, TN: Sword of the Word Publishers, 1989), 304.

Chapter 6
Participating in God's Plan Through Prayer

God's eternal plan has been moving forward from the foundation of the world. Because God loves and desires fellowship with human beings, He has chosen to involve believers in His redemptive plan for humankind and has purposed to bring us to glory to rule with Him forever. In this study you have seen ways God has used the prayers of His saints, like Moses, Paul, and many others, to shape history according to His grand design.

Prayer in our lives today is a significant way God shapes us for His use now and through eternity. As a believer you have the privilege of entering His presence and allowing Him to change your heart and bring you into conformity to the likeness of His Son. You also have the thrilling responsibility to join God's purposes as you pray for His will to be done and for His kingdom to come on earth. In this final chapter you will consider ways you can participate in God's plan through your prayers with your church, with your family, and in your personal time with God.

Prayer in our lives today is a significant way God shapes us for His use now and through eternity.

Prayer in the Early Church

If we examine the church's expansion in the Book of Acts and look at its prayers as recorded in Acts and the Epistles, we see convincing proof of the power of prayer. The early church had innumerable obstacles: Christianity was unknown, it was opposed by the authorities wherever it spread, it constantly suffered from false accusations and rumors, and it tended to attract the lower classes. Yet by the end of the first century, it had spread in exactly the geographical pattern commissioned by Jesus—Jerusalem, Judea, Samaria, and the "uttermost part of the earth" (Acts 1:8, KJV)—points in Europe and Asia Minor far distant from its seedbed.

The expansion was such that it paved the way for an entirely new pattern of divine work, hardly conceivable in Judaism. This rapid geographical and ideological shift could have been accomplished only by supernatural forces. The instrument of expansion was the church, and the force the church used was prayer. Paul was one of the primary tools, but thousands of Christians scattered by the persecution were also used. These became firebrands to ignite the fire of divine heat all over the Mediterranean world. Many of those firebrands had learned the divine method in Jerusalem, where prayer saturated the work of that first Christian church.

The Early Churches Prayed for Guidance

The birth of the church occurred in an atmosphere of prayer and praise. After the ascension the disciples "returned to Jerusalem with great joy, and were continually in the temple, praising God" (Luke 24:52-53). This evidently was not private prayer, and it provided the climate for an ongoing community lifestyle of praying together. Much of that prayer was probably prayer for the Lord's guidance.

"Thou art my Rock and my fortress; For Thy name's sake Thou wilt lead me and guide me" (Ps. 31:3).

The Old Testament precedent was to look to God for guidance. It was an important part of Jewish history; the psalmist often sang of divine leadership (see Pss. 23:2-3; 31:3). Many songs sang of God's guidance toward Canaan. The Levites' song after the new celebration of the Feast of Tabernacles on their return to Jerusalem from captivity acknowledged that their guidance was from ancient days:

> *The pillar of cloud did not leave them by day,*
> *To guide them on their way,*
> *Nor the pillar of fire by night, to light for them the way*
> *   in which they were to go (Neh. 9:19).*

Zacharias's prophecy had said that the coming Messiah would " 'guide our feet into the way of peace' " (Luke 1:79). Jesus had promised that the Holy Spirit would guide into all truth (see John 16:13). God would guide the church, as He had always guided Israel. In this bracing atmosphere of buoyant expectation, the church prayed for guidance in the selection of a replacement for Judas among the twelve: " 'Thou, Lord, who knowest the hearts of all men, show which one of these two [Joseph or Matthias] Thou hast chosen' " (Acts 1:24).

Guidance was important to the infant church. It did not yet have the New Testament Scriptures for help and instruction. Ahead of it lay expansion on a scale unimaginable at that time, miracles, persecution, separation, and scattering. Unaware of the proportions of the monumental task ahead of it, the church turned to prayer, guided by the experience of the history of Israel; its spiritual instincts; and, above all, the Holy Spirit Himself. He had been promised in Jesus' last discourse, and they had been commanded to wait on His empowering (see Luke 24:49). Christ's final word before He ascended was that they would receive power when the Holy Spirit came upon them (see Acts 1:8).

From the events in Acts 2 on, God's guidance was specifically the guidance of the Holy Spirit. The entire apostolic record indicates that the church looked to Him as guide, prayed with His specific guidance in mind, and credited Him with being the fullness of God working in them. He became the instrument of spiritual birth and spiritual work, He protected the church in danger, and He initiated the church's great missionary expansion.

The Early Churches Were Places of Prayer

Repeatedly, Luke records the early church as being of one mind or of one heart (see Acts 1:14; 2:46; 4:32). This unity is the basis of Paul's appeal to the Corinthian church to understand the interworking of the parts of the body (see 1 Cor. 12—14). He told them, "If one member suffers, all the members suffer with it; if one member is honored, all the members rejoice with it" (1 Cor. 12:26). The church was an organism, with interdependent parts that needed one another to function properly. Later, Paul would entreat the church at Ephesus to be "diligent to preserve the unity of the Spirit in the bond of peace" (Eph. 4:3).

This bond secures awesome authority with God. Read Jesus' words in the margin. A believer is the temple of the Holy Spirit (see 1 Cor. 6:19). When two of these temples filled with the Holy Spirit gather, a new and even more powerful expression of the presence of Christ Himself works outward with fearsome energy.

As the disciples awaited the Spirit's coming after Christ's ascension, "these all with one mind were continually devoting themselves to prayer, along with the women, and Mary the mother of Jesus, and with His brothers" (Acts 1:14). That was the atmosphere that prepared the way for Pentecost! After Pentecost brought the first great ingathering, that same atmosphere continued: "They were continually devoting themselves to the apostles' teaching and to fellowship, to the breaking of bread and to prayer" (Acts 2:42).

" 'If two of you agree on earth about anything that they may ask, it shall be done for them by My Father who is in heaven. For where two or three have gathered together in My name, there I am in their midst' " (Matt. 18:19-20).

No wonder "everyone kept feeling a sense of awe; and many wonders and signs were taking place through the apostles" (Acts 2:43)!

Isaiah's ancient epithet of the temple as a "house of prayer" (Isa. 56:7) was being fully realized in the new household of God. Paul called this new body the "temple of God," where God's own Spirit dwelt (1 Cor. 3:16; the pronoun in this verse is plural). The life of this body was mediated through prayer, and the dominant spirit of that continuing prayer was praise (see Acts 2:47).

The fact that prayer was the apostles' central activity is shown by the resolution of the conflict in Acts 6. The seven men selected to distribute food were chosen so that the apostles could devote themselves to prayer and the ministry of the word (see Acts 6:4). After the men were chosen, they were set aside by prayer (see Acts 6:6).

Wherever Christianity found a nesting place, that place rapidly became a place of prayer.

When Paul and his party arrived in Philippi, they began by looking for "a place of prayer," and it was there, in the place of prayer, that the first European church was born (Acts 16:13-15). Later, the Philippian jailer was converted as God worked through the midnight prayers of Paul and Silas (see Acts 16:25-33). The churches of the first century did not need to debate the importance of prayer; they naturally turned to prayer. Wherever Christianity found a nesting place, that place rapidly became a place of prayer, and Christ's presence, through the power of the Holy Spirit, began working outward from the assembled body of new believers.

Prayer Sustained the Early Church in Crisis

Soon after the inception of the new body, danger confronted its members. Peter and John had been instruments for healing a crippled beggar at the gate of the temple; the reaction provided Peter with an opportunity for a convincing sermon, whereupon he and John were arrested. They then presented an unanswerable argument to the Sanhedrin, and the Sanhedrin, helpless to dispute the sermon and the events, released the two men but warned them not to teach or speak in Jesus' name. The church immediately went to prayer and eloquently asked for boldness of speech. "When they had prayed, the place where they had gathered together was shaken, and they were all filled with the Holy Spirit, and began to speak the word of God with boldness" (Acts 4:31).

After that, continuing danger was an invitation to continuing prayer. Herod Agrippa I discovered that persecuting the church pleased the Jewish leaders, so he executed James, John's brother, and imprisoned Peter. The church fervently prayed, and Peter was miraculously delivered (see Acts 12:5-11). Danger would always accompany the spread of the church and its work. The letter of the Jerusalem church to the church at Antioch to resolve the question over circumcision described its bearers, Paul, Barnabas, Judas called Barsabbas, and Silas, as "men who have risked their lives for the name of our Lord Jesus Christ" (Acts 15:26). Paul wrote the Corinthians that he was "in danger every hour" (1 Cor. 15:30) and later described to them a wide variety of dangers and circumstances he endured—imprisonment, lashing, beating, stoning, shipwreck, near drowning, and betrayal (see 2 Cor. 11:23-26). Persecution hounded the early Christians on every hand, and they quickly found that the one reliable resource they could revert to was prayer.

Through prayer, blessing and fruit resulted from the very factors that threatened the church. Imprisoned at Philippi, Paul and Silas "were praying and singing hymns of praise to God" (Acts 16:25), and the miraculous earthquake that followed enabled Paul to speak a word that brought the jailer to Christ. The participants in that continuing first-century drama knew that without prayer they could not have survived, nor could they have propagated the faith.

Through prayer, blessing and fruit resulted from the very factors that threatened the church.

Prayer Fueled the Missions Movement

In prayer, as in salvation, the initiative is with God. It is God who leads, God who opens. There is a clear indication that the missionary movement was initiated first in the hearts of the missionaries to be sent, then in the church that was to send them. It began in Antioch, where a mighty group of prophets and teachers was assembled: "While they were ministering to the Lord and fasting, the Holy Spirit said, 'Set apart for Me Barnabas and Saul for the work to which I have called them' " (Acts 13:2). This seems to indicate that Barnabas and Saul already knew they had been called. Now the Holy Spirit called the church to send them.

The two were sent with prayer: "When they had fasted and prayed and laid their hands on them, they sent them away" (Acts 13:3). The next verse describes the church's expansion as seen in the rest of the Book of Acts: "... being sent out by the Holy Spirit." With prayer the believers exported a new faith, born in Judaism, outside the borders of Israel. The Holy Spirit initiated the missions movement in prayer, communicated to all of the participants in prayer, and carried out what He had instigated through prayer.

"When they had appointed elders for them in every church, having prayed with fasting, they commended them to the Lord in whom they had believed" (Acts 14:23).

Prayer continued to be an important factor in the church's ongoing mission. On the return part of their first missionary journey, Paul and Barnabas revisited churches they had established (see Acts 14:23). Prayer greatly contributed to the founding of the Philippian church (see Acts 16:16,25). When Paul met with the Ephesian elders at Miletus, "he knelt down and prayed with them all" (Acts 20:36). As he left Tyre, the entire congregation accompanied him to the ship and prayed with him (see Acts 21:5).

Most conclusive of all, however, are the numerous teachings on prayer in the Epistles, the recorded prayers of Paul, and the requests made by him for the churches' prayers. The abundant references to prayer in Paul's letters appear chronologically throughout his journeys as he planted churches in Asia Minor and Europe.

Read the following verses and name examples of things Paul prayed for the early churches.

Ephesians 3:16-19 _____

_____

Colossians 1:9-12 _____

_____

Read the following verses and name things Paul asked the early churches to pray for him.

Ephesians 6:19-20 _____

_____

2 Thessalonians 3:1-2 _____

_____

Paul constantly gave thanks to God for the churches. He prayed that the believers would live in harmony and unity with one another, that they would live good lives and grow to maturity in Christ, that God would give them wisdom and understanding and power, that Christ would dwell in their hearts, that they might comprehend the greatness of God's love, that their love would overflow for others, that they would be inwardly clean, that their lives would be pleasing to God, that they would minister to others, and that he could see the believers again to minister to them.

Paul asked the Christians to pray for him also—that he would be protected from hostile unbelievers in Jerusalem, that he would be able to preach the gospel with boldness, that he would have opportunities to preach the gospel even while in prison, and that the Word of God would spread.

Prayer was the life of the church, its breath. Spiritual work was done with spiritual resources.

Prayer in the Church Today

When Paul gave Timothy instructions for pastoring the church at Ephesus, he left us valuable information on public worship: "First of all, then, I urge that entreaties and prayers, petitions and thanksgivings, be made on behalf of all men, for kings and all who are in authority, in order that we may lead a tranquil and quiet life in all godliness and dignity" (1 Tim. 2:1-2). This is written for practice by the church. Later, he would enjoin public prayer again (see v. 8).

Even if the early church had not followed the Hebrew pattern of worship, the psalms would have remained important throughout Christian history. Hymns and spiritual songs played a major part (see Eph. 5:19; Col. 3:16) and were, of course, closely related to prayer. The pattern of dependence on prayer as the foundation of and basis for safety, fellowship in the unity of the Spirit, and expansion of the body has remained. Public prayer should always be a vital part of the church's worship.

Prayer together. The church must pray together, with mutuality of spirit. Although prayer rooms and prayer chains greatly contribute to a church's life, there is no substitute for praying together. Mutual prayer distributes the church's burdens so that all can carry the work of prayer home for the rest of the week. Prayer binds the church together as nothing else can. Most congregations sing together but do little else together. The greater part of the usual public service, Sunday or midweek, is spent passively listen-

"Our Lord has said that where two or three gather in His name, He is there. What would happen if the average prayer meeting at church should ever take that seriously and believe it? Instead, we pray, 'Lord be with us' when He is already with us! Instead, we ought to shout, 'Look who's here!' "[1]
—Vance Havner (1901–86), evangelist who preached the gospel for 72 years

ing to a preacher, a soloist, or a choir. We worship with the soloist or choir, and we receive spiritual insight from the preacher, but it is equally important for the church to agree in prayer.

Prayer of intercession. Intercessory prayer especially must be a regular activity of the church. Paul's plea to the Roman church for prayer is addressed to them in the plural—the entire church was being asked to pray for him (see Rom. 15:30). He made similar requests to the Ephesians (see Eph. 6:19), to the Thessalonians (see 1 Thess. 5:25), and to other churches. No doubt there was much private and small-group prayer also; that would have been consistent with the atmosphere of the time. Paul's own prayers brighten the pages of his letters.

Prayer for guidance. The church family should also pray for guidance in its ongoing ministry. Because Christ is the head (see Eph. 5:23), we must look to Him. He expects His sheep to recognize His voice and follow Him (see John 10:2-4). What we are to pray for in the church's ongoing ministry is well documented in Paul's prayers for the churches (see Eph. 3:14-19; Col. 1:9-12; also see chap. 3 for more on these).

Prayer for Christ's work. The church should pray for Christ's work everywhere. The universality of the churches' concern is shown in their wide sharing with one another, sometimes across considerable geographical distance. The church of Syrian Antioch shared with the Judean Christians (see Acts 11:29). Paul directed the Corinthians to make a "collection for the saints" in Jerusalem (1 Cor. 16:1). He told them that the Macedonians generously shared of their means (see 2 Cor. 8:1-5). Not only were they to share in needs, but they were also to participate by means of prayer in the work of all the saints. The word *all* pervades the injunction to the Ephesians to pray: "With all prayer and petition pray at all times in the Spirit, and ... be on the alert with all perseverance and petition for all the saints" (Eph. 6:18). Provincialism could not dominate the thinking of this new people of God, as it had in Judaism. Their world was as big as the one God had placed them in.

The church today has more control over the course of this world than any civic authority or power. Any spiritual prayer in Jesus' name carries tremendous authority. In the unified prayer of Christians together that authority wields unimaginable power. The work of God and the advance of the kingdom are in the hands of the church.

> *" 'He who enters by the door is a shepherd of the sheep. To him the doorkeeper opens, and the sheep hear his voice, and he calls his own sheep by name, and leads them out. When he puts forth all his own, he goes before them, and the sheep follow him because they know his voice' " (John 10:2-4).*

Make prayer lists for the needs of your church.

Church Leaders	Members in Need
_____	_____
_____	_____
_____	_____
_____	_____
Church Ministries	**World Missions**
_____	_____
_____	_____
_____	_____
_____	_____

"Lord, … help me to realize the unity of the race and the universality of thy mission of redemption. Lord, help me to feel that Paradise is roomy and in my Father's house are many mansions; that it will not crowd or jostle me if from every tribe and tongue and kindred the blood-washed may come."[2] —B. H. Carroll (1843–1914), founder and first president of Southwestern Baptist Theological Seminary

Stop and pray for the persons and work you listed. Transfer the lists to your prayer notebook. Commit yourself to pray daily for the needs and persons listed.

Prayer in the Home

The title of God that Jesus gave us to use in our prayers—Father—suggests something of His view of the home and its role. Paul was later to call the body of believers the "household of the faith" (Gal. 6:10) and "God's household" (Eph. 2:19). That figure of speech and the name *Father* for *God* originated in an ideal familiar to Judaism—a family with strong, loving, caring parents and children who were loyal and representative of parental training.

Homes and households were important in the Gospels. The devout household of Zacharias and Elizabeth provided the environment for shaping John the Baptist. The home of Zebedee, Salome, James, and John furnished Christ with love and followers. When Andrew perceived Christ's identity, "he found first his own brother Simon, and said to him, 'We have found the Messiah' "

(John 1:41). Jesus found refuge in the home of Mary, Martha, and Lazarus. Because He visited often, their home must have refreshed Him, and John recorded that He loved them deeply (see John 11:5).

Conversion to Christianity in New Testament times often took place by family blocks. Jesus told Zaccheus, " 'Today salvation has come to this house' " (Luke 19:9). A plural number were baptized in the remarkable conversion account of Cornelius (see Acts 10: 47-48). The Philippian jailer's entire household came to the Lord at one time (see Acts 16:33). Family households often became the meeting place of a local church (see Rom. 16:5; Philem. 2).

It was natural that the Christian community adopted the Jewish standard for homes. The strength of the home provided Jesus with a figure of speech to indicate the incongruity of a divided family's remaining strong. He was actually stating His own unity with the Spirit of God and, by implication, the strength of a unified household (see Matt. 12:25). Married couples were to demonstrate solidarity and unity of purpose, especially in their prayers. Peter's command for husbands to live considerately with their wives implied an understanding that their unified prayers would accomplish much. This prayer force must not be impeded (see 1 Pet. 3:7).

As I was pastoring a church on an interim basis in the spring of 1985, I tried to develop a spirit of prayer in that body by example and teaching. In the first Wednesday-evening service I asked each of the 67 members present to fill out a card stating his or her greatest prayer needs. I explained that the card would be for private use by me alone. I then took those cards and prayed daily for each person according to the needs mentioned. We began to see an unusual work of the Lord. In spite of a prayerful spirit that grew in the body and a beautiful self-giving that many in the church exhibited, I discovered early that only a few of the families were practicing family devotions. After that, in ministering to many churches and seminary students, I began to uncover the fact that the family altar, as my family always called it, is exceedingly rare among Christians—even among ministers and leaders.

The usual excuse people make about having family devotions is that they cannot find a time when all the family remains still together for a few minutes. Time, of course, is a major problem in the hectic diversity of activities—church, business, sports, television, education—that most families maintain. There can be no question that time is a serious, difficult, major problem in sched-

"I believe there are many in our parishes who do not make a habit of secret prayer—who, neither in their closet nor in the embowering shade, ever pour out their heart to God."[3]
—*Robert Murray McCheyne (1813–43), Scottish pastor*

uling regular family devotions. But the lack of mutual prayer together is a more serious, difficult, and weighty problem. Families will not establish the practice of family devotions until they become convinced that it is more important than their other activities. The problem of prayerless families is probably only a symptom of the larger problem of prayerless people.

Perhaps what we need are models. If, in the churches where this book is taught, godly men and women would determine that their families could become models for other families, a movement might develop. I would like to suggest that the pastor and his wife in every church firmly commit their home to family prayer and enlist other spiritual leaders in the church to do the same.

Several people have confessed to me that they do not have family devotions because they are self-conscious about it. Often the father has said that he feels he is supposed to be a teacher in that situation but that he is embarrassed because his wife knows more about the Bible than he. Both the husband and the wife must support prayer in the home. Neither should assume a superior or demanding attitude. Each should help the other as they provide spiritual leadership for the family and create opportunities for the family to learn and worship together.

I have been part of a family altar all my life. My parents established the pattern of family devotions before I was born. Every evening as I grew up, we would gather in the living room, talk about our day, read the Bible together, and pray. I vividly remember my parents thanking the Lord nightly for their two sons and asking His guidance as they trained us for kingdom service. Prayer came naturally to my brother and me because we never knew life apart from it. That daily altar time highlighted the centrality of Christ's reign in our home. It also provided us with a security that has never been shaken and a faith in the reality of divine provision and protection in all circumstances.

My wife and I established the practice of family devotions together more than a year before we married. That, in turn, led to other family traditions—a family psalm, a family hymn, annual home Thanksgiving services, and other meaningful experiences. My wife's cancer and chemotherapy revealed new, convincing proofs of the power of a strong married bond that validates the promise of Scripture. The stronger the bond, the more powerful and efficacious the prayer! As far back as my daughter and my grandchildren

Families will not establish the practice of family devotions until they become convinced that it is more important than their other activities.

can remember, home was a happy, praying place, a strong refuge with Christ at the center, Christ made manifest by prayer.

Our family altar is a time of mutual sharing. After we read a Bible passage together, we each share and prayerfully discuss ideas about what we have read, our life together, the church, events in the Lord's work that our prayers might touch, or family and friends who need prayer. We do not feel obligated to pose wise solutions or appear spiritual. We simply talk. For us, it is never formal or fussy, self-conscious or posed, just friendly, with the interest vested in God's glory and the progress of His work. Then each of us prays. Sometimes one of us prays a long prayer or an unusually heartfelt prayer, but there is never an ensuing obligation to match the quality of anyone else's prayer. There is great freedom simply to be ourselves. The family altar is no time to prove anything.

We have found the early morning to be ideal for family devotions. We usually rise early, eat a simple breakfast, and enjoy our time together with the Lord.

> *A morning devotional time gives me a security about my day that is irreplaceable.*

A morning devotional time gives me a security about my day that is irreplaceable. By the time I begin the day's activities, I have realized anew that God is still on His throne. I have also experienced a sense of His love for me and His provision for my day's needs. I have secured the endorsement of my wife's prayers, and I know that she will continue to pray for me throughout the day.

If a family cannot manage an early-morning time, the evening might work. A television program is not much to sacrifice for the eternal value of time with the Lord. The best time would be just before bedtime. I grew up with a family time each evening, and it greatly contributed to my spiritual growth and sense of security.

Describe the way your family devotions are conducted.

_____

_____

Evaluate your practice of family devotions in light of what you have just read. List ideas for making your devotions more meaningful for each family member.

_____

_____

_____

_____

Prayer in the Believer's Life

The prayer life of every Christian will bear a unique mold because the prayer calling of every Christian is unique. Each prayer warrior of the Bible had prayer patterns peculiar to himself or herself. Every Christian should determine through prayer the one pattern and purpose that God wants to use in his or her life.

Prayer That Is Shaped by the Word
Prayer—and for that matter, all our thought life—needs the shape of the mind of Christ. The most effective tool we have for shaping our thoughts is God's thoughts as they are revealed in the Bible. Regular reading of the Bible exposes our minds to God's thoughts. The more exposure we give our minds to the Bible, provided it is interpreted according to Christ's example and teaching, the more likely we are to be conformed to the pattern of Christ's character.

*"The words of the Lord
are pure words;
As silver tried in a furnace
on the earth, refined
seven times" (Ps. 12:6).*

Rate your personal prayer life by circling your responses. 1 = very seldom; 3 = sometimes; 5 = often.

I have a daily devotional time.	1	2	3	4	5
Prayer is an integral part of my devotions.	1	2	3	4	5
I include Bible reading in my devotional activity.	1	2	3	4	5
I maintain an active prayer list.	1	2	3	4	5
I pray for others as well as for my own needs.	1	2	3	4	5
I pray for each member of my family.	1	2	3	4	5

I pray for my pastor and other church leaders.	1	2	3	4	5
I pray for my church family.	1	2	3	4	5
I pray for missionaries and for Christ's work around the world.	1	2	3	4	5
I pray for persecuted Christians.	1	2	3	4	5
I pray for the leaders of my country.	1	2	3	4	5
I receive specific answers to my prayers.	1	2	3	4	5

What changes do you need to make for your devotional life to be more effective and meaningful?

_____

_____

Years ago in my devotions I gave large blocks of time to prayer and only a few minutes to Bible study. Then I heard E. F. Hallock, well known for his teaching on prayer, state that we should not have to choose between time in the Bible and time in prayer but that if a choice has to be made, it is more important that God speak to an individual than that a person speak to God. That statement reformed my prayer life, not only in the amount of time I allotted to studying and meditating on Scripture but also in the very tenure of my prayers, as I found myself increasingly being shaped by the words of Scripture that lodged in my subconscious.

The ancient practice of meditating on Scripture should form an important part of our devotional life. The Lord told Joshua: " 'This book of the law shall not depart from your mouth, but you shall meditate on it day and night, so that you may be careful to do according to all that is written in it; for then you will make your way prosperous, and then you will have success' " (Josh. 1:8). We enjoy what we are familiar with; and we choose what we will be familiar with. Here are some ways Scripture shapes your prayer life.

Scripture quickens its hearers. Scripture enlivens our desire for the things of God and satisfies the yearning for God that is natural to a Christian. When Jesus explained Scripture to Cleopas and his companion on the road to Emmaus, they exclaimed to one

"Thy words were found and I ate them, And Thy words became for me a joy and the delight of my heart; For I have been called by Thy name, O Lord God of hosts" (Jer. 15:16).

another, " 'Were not our hearts burning within us while He was speaking to us on the road, while He was explaining the Scriptures to us?' " (Luke 24:32). The Holy Spirit is our teacher today as we read God's Word, just as Jesus was Cleopas's teacher, and believers commonly sense a burning intensity within as the Holy Spirit brings insight to Scripture.

Scripture is a teacher. It enlightens our minds and illuminates the roadway we follow. The psalmist declared:

> *From Thy precepts I get understanding;*
> *Therefore I hate every false way.*
> *Thy word is a lamp to my feet,*
> *And a light to my path (Ps. 119:104-105).*

God has a special blessing for those who learn from His law:

> *Blessed is the man whom Thou dost chasten, O Lord,*
> *And dost teach out of Thy law (Ps. 94:12).*

Many times I have started the day with a heavy burden, only to find such joy in discoveries in the Bible that my prayers became surprisingly buoyant.

Scripture clarifies God's intention. The Sadducees did not believe in resurrection and, attempting to trick Jesus, posed an absurd, complicated story about a woman being married seven times to different brothers. Their question about whose wife she would be in the resurrection confused the spiritual nature of the resurrection life. Jesus told them, " 'You are mistaken, not understanding the Scriptures, or the power of God' " (Matt. 22:29). We can understand the Scriptures only if we understand God's power and interpret them in faith.

Scripture points to Christ as the center of our faith. The Old Testament prepared for the work of Christ. When the Jews were angered because Jesus called God His Father (see John 5:18), He made several sweeping claims about the nature of His relationship with the Father and concluded these with references to several witnesses about Himself—the witness of John the Baptist, the witness of His own works, the witness of the Father, and the witness of Scripture. He told them, " 'You search the Scriptures, because you think that in them you have eternal life; and it is these that bear

"One of the greatest privileges of the child of God is the privilege of coming directly to God in prayer."[4]
—*Billy Graham, evangelist*

133

witness of Me' " (John 5:39). Later, the apostle John was to say of his own Gospel, "These have been written that you may believe that Jesus is the Christ, the Son of God; and that believing you may have life in His name" (John 20:31).

A Time and a Place for Prayer

The concepts of the tabernacle, the temple, and prescribed feasts of the year support the idea of establishing a regular time and place for our devotions, although, of course, being governed by a new and better testament, we are never slaves to the idea that God is limited by any building, creed, or institution.

A time for prayer. The greatest men and women of spiritual history have preferred the early morning for their regular devotional exercises. However, if the morning is impossible for you, choose another time of day to reserve for focused conversation with the Father. Keep this time as you would any other appointment.

A place for prayer. I have a prayer room in my home and have found a kneeling altar to be very helpful. My wife and I have had kneeling altars made for our grandchildren. As adults they can use them in their weddings, if they marry, and as reminders of the importance of prayer in their lives.

Prayer tools. A prayer list can help you cover all the areas for which you need to pray. The writer of Ecclesiastes advised, "Do not be hasty in word or impulsive in thought to bring up a matter in the presence of God" (Eccl. 5:2). Organizing our thoughts in prayer is one means of demonstrating and maintaining reverence. Hosea even suggested taking our repentance to God with the clarity of thought-out words:

> *Take words with you and return to the Lord.*
> *Say to Him, "Take away all iniquity,*
> *And receive us graciously,*
> *That we may present the fruit of our lips" (Hos. 14:2).*

A notebook for prayer needs and guidance is useful in organizing and scheduling prayers. I maintain the following lists in my notebook.

"In the morning, O Lord, Thou wilt hear my voice; In the morning I will order my prayer to Thee and eagerly watch" (Ps. 5:3).

Daily List—Permanent

People for whom I pray every day:
- All family members
- My pastor and staff
- My daughter's pastor
- Several close friends
- Other continuing concerns

Daily List—Temporary

Concerns that change from time to time:
- The writing of this book
- Sick friends
- Lost persons I have recently met

Weekly List

Under each day of the week I list the following.
- Friends
- Concerns
- Denominational agencies
- Agency officials
- Denominational officers
- Missionaries
- Governments and government officials

Monthly List

Each day of the month I pray for other items that are important but somewhat remote from my immediate situation.

"George Mueller kept a record of his praying ... whether it was a little request or a big one he entered it, and when the answer came he wrote down the answer and the date. At the time of his death his friends went through these records and counted more than fifty thousand definite answers to specific petitions offered by this man."[5]
—*"Preacher" E. F. Hallock (1888–1978), pastor of First Baptist Church; Norman, Oklahoma*

For many of these concerns I write appropriate Scriptures in my notebook. For example, I quote to the Lord Scriptures that apply to a Christian wife as I pray for my wife (see Prov. 31:10-31; Eph. 5:22-24), and I use Scriptures on the biblical qualifications of a pastor to pray for my pastor (see 1 Tim. 3:1-7; 2 Tim. 4:1-2; Titus 1:5-9). In addition, it has been helpful to maintain a list of divine statements and promises that may be used in various prayer situations (see 2 Chron. 7:14; 16:9; Isa. 43:1-2; Jer. 32:27).

Very encouraging to my faith has been a list of answered prayers. I do not record every prayer and every answer, but certain prayers and answers have proved to be so instructive that I record them so that the lesson will not be lost. This list goes back to 1943!

I do not follow my lists slavishly, but I find them to be good general guides to prevent prayer from assuming a selfish orientation, to aid my memory (the mind should pray as well as the spirit), and to assign an order of importance to the things for which I should pray.

But there are delightful free periods in my own quiet time when I joyfully follow the Holy Spirit in many matters—concerns, praise, and thanksgiving. For me, maintaining a prayer list represents my desire not to appear before God empty-handed (see Ex. 34:20).

During my wife's chemotherapy we gathered so many new insights that we recorded the understandings and the Scriptures that were comforting and instructive. We spent many hours together and separately exploring the profound insights that grew from Paul's sufferings, especially those recorded in 2 Corinthians.

Posture may make a difference in attitude. Paul bowed his knees, indicating humility (see Eph. 3:14). The elders in the great heavenly scene in Revelation fell on their faces in prostrate adoration (see Rev. 11:16). Almost any reverent posture is appropriate, but it helps when your body participates in offering prayer to God.

Anytime, anywhere. An attitude of prayer at any time or any place should be cultivated. We are to "pray without ceasing" (1 Thess. 5:17); the only physical activity we carry on ceaselessly is the act of breathing. In prayer we breathe spiritually; this command shows how essential prayer is in the spiritual life. It means that there is no place so unholy that we cannot pray in it. It means that there is no time in which we can afford to ignore God.

It is discourteous to ignore someone who is with you, and Jesus Himself assured us of His continuing presence (see Matt. 28:20). He later said to Paul in Corinth, " 'Do not be afraid any longer, but go on speaking and do not be silent; for I am with you' " (Acts 18:9-10). Can you imagine Paul ignoring that gracious courtesy? When we ignore Christ, we insult Him.

Admittedly, it is difficult to remember to pray during most of our hectic days. As you are learning, it would be helpful to set aside brief periods for prayer at intervals through the day as a reminder. If you ask God to remind you, He will do so. Certainly, a brief prayer at bedtime is necessary. I also try to use my environment to remind me. For example, sometimes I dress in colors that suggest divine attributes—white of purity, green of life, red of sacrifice, and purple of royalty. Then as I go through the day, the colors I am wearing remind me of God's presence in my life.

Prayer may be aloud (see Rev. 5:12) or silent (see 1 Sam. 1:13). It may be in a home (see Acts 10:9) or on a beach (see Acts 21:5). It may be at midnight (see Acts 16:25) or in the morning (see Ps. 5:3). It may be for a child (Hannah; 1 Sam. 1:11), for life (Hezekiah;

> *"We should make much of secret prayer. Nothing should crowd it out. Nothing should be substituted for it. We should have a special time for secret prayer. It should be made a habit and become as vital and as necessary as our meals."*[6]
> —*L. R. Scarborough (1870–1945), evangelist and president of Southwestern Baptist Theological Seminary*

2 Kings 20:3), or for boldness (the church after Pentecost; Acts 4:29). Prayer may be made anywhere, anytime, for any holy purpose—and ought to be.

Willingness in Prayer

A willingness to accept and do God's will should undergird prayer. Jesus' own " 'Not as I will, but as Thou wilt' " (Matt. 26:39) is the eternal standard for any relationship with God. It is not the formula " 'Thy will be done' " (Matt. 6:10) that secures divine action; rather, the relationship that grows from that attitude enables us to pray within God's will and places us within the framework where His power is active.

Willingness automatically rules out rebellion, anger, and bitterness if our prayers are not answered as we would like for them to be. Such attitudes are not conducive to a prayer relationship and indicate hostility toward God. If we pray for something that God, in His wisdom, knows He cannot give, we may be assured that our ultimate happiness is as important to Him as it is to us. Temporary disappointment may mean eternal gladness.

Willingness in prayer is saying to God: "I think I know what is best, but I know that You know what is best. I prefer Your judgment to mine." It is acknowledging that God is wiser than we are. It is agreeing that His purposes are grander than ours. It is admitting that our small part of the picture does not include larger designs over a wide canvas that we cannot see.

Willingness does not preclude disappointment and hurt. In the loss of someone we love very much, God is not angry if we mourn or express our sense of loss. He is sympathetic when we hurt. Isaiah wrote of God's mercies on Israel, "In all their affliction He was afflicted" (Isa. 63:9). He heard the groaning of the children of Israel (see Ex. 2:24).

Willingness means that we always participate in God's greater purposes, as Christ did in His Gethsemane prayer (see Matt. 26:36-46). It means that the purposes of our lives are not temporal but eternal. It means that when we hurt, rather than turning from God, we turn to Him and allow Him to comfort us and help us grow through duress, stress, and loss. Our hurt provides God with an opportunity to give Himself more fully to us. Our willingness in prayer means that we are becoming more like Him.

"The Lord is gracious
and merciful;
Slow to anger and great
in lovingkindness"
(Ps. 145:8).

Listening to God

In all three recorded conversations between Noah and God, Noah is pictured as listening. "Noah walked with God" (Gen. 6:9), and yet it was God who did the talking. Repeatedly, the record states that God spoke to Noah (see Gen. 6:13; 7:1; 8:15; 9:1,8,17). Noah always responded to the Lord with obedience (see Gen. 6:22; 7:5; 8:18). Can there be any wonder that "God remembered Noah" (Gen. 8:1) or that "God blessed Noah and his sons" (Gen. 9:1)? Noah walked with God by listening to Him and obeying Him.

How do we listen to God? The clearest way is by knowing His Word.

How do we listen to God? The clearest way is by knowing His Word. God will not work in patterns foreign to the patterns revealed in the Bible. To know the mind of Christ today, it is helpful to be familiar with the way He expressed it in His incarnation. We must know His steps and learn to recognize His kind of steps.

Troubled not only by the depth of Judah's sin but also by the Lord's use of the Babylonians to punish Judah, Habakkuk asked God to explain this strange use of wickedness to punish God's people, even in their unrighteousness. He said,

> *I will stand on my guard post*
> *And station myself on the rampart;*
> *And I will keep watch to see what He will speak to me (Hab. 2:1).*

Habakkuk wanted to hear from God and was willing to watch for the answer. Watchfulness or alertness is a part of hearing God; God answered Habakkuk (see Hab. 2:2). We must be willing, sensitive, and alert. Long ago another man of God said,

> *I will hear what God the Lord will say;*
> *For He will speak peace to His people, to His godly ones (Ps. 85:8).*

I have found it helpful to keep a record of important requests of God and to document the way He works as I pray. That documentation has been very instructive. God works with me today as He has worked with me in the past. I have also compared the kind of the things He does for me and in me with the kind of things He did in the biblical record. There is an amazing correspondence, which validates His unchanging nature and provides me with security in knowing what to expect.

I also find that in discerning the Lord's leadership, I can trust

138

impressions born in submissive prayer and Bible study oriented to the lordship of Christ. I have learned to be suspicious of impressions born in moments of urgency, irritation, anger, unresolved guilt, or sin. God works with spirits that are sensitive to His.

Disobeying the known will of God is courting disaster. One of the saddest moments in the historical record occurred during the reign of Hoshea, the last king of Israel: "The king of Assyria carried Israel away into exile to Assyria … because they did not obey the voice of the Lord their God, but transgressed His covenant, even all that Moses the servant of the Lord commanded; they would neither listen, nor do it" (2 Kings 18:11-12). This refusal to hear came at the end of a long record of disobedience. The Bible's commands are given for obedience, which garners protection and blessing. Disobedience is a strange alternative for a Christian.

Expectancy in Prayer

Hope is one of the most misunderstood words in the New Testament. It means that by faith we start enjoying now what we know is coming; hope is present pleasure in a future blessing. Hope is expectant; it presents a bright face to God.

Expectancy in prayer should be based on the truth and promises of God's Word. The ultimate validity of prayer does not depend on human faith but on God's Word. He honors His own Word. He magnifies His Word in accordance with His own name, all that it identifies, all that it specifies (see Ps. 138:8). The most secure thing in the world is truth.

Truth enables waiting. We can wait only if expectancy characterizes our walk and prayers. Psalm 25:5 conveys that note of expectancy:

Lead me in Thy truth and teach me,
For Thou art the God of my salvation;
For Thee I wait all the day.

Paul had a radiant expectancy: "I know that this shall turn out for my deliverance [from prison] through your prayers and the provision of the Spirit of Jesus Christ, according to my earnest expectation and hope, that I shall not be put to shame in anything, but that with all boldness, Christ shall even now, as always, be exalted in my body, whether by life or by death" (Phil. 1:19-20).

Waiting can be excruciating if our hope is worldly. Waiting on

> *"The Lord will accomplish*
> *what concerns me;*
> *Thy lovingkindness,*
> *O Lord, is everlasting;*
> *Do not forsake the works*
> *of Thy hands"*
> *(Ps. 138:8).*

Waiting on God is restful if we fully understand that it is God we are waiting on.

God is restful if we fully understand that it is God we are waiting on. Again, the psalmist said,

> *My soul, wait in silence for God only,*
> *For my hope is from Him (Ps. 62:5).*

There is no anxiety in that expectant hope; all is quietness and rest. Expectancy does not fidget; yet it enjoys the energy that comes from faith.

Assume that a new believer is talking with you about prayer. Respond to her in the boxes provided.

"I've prayed and prayed, but it has done no good. I don't see the point in continuing to pray."

"I am willing to accept and do God's will if He would just make it known to me. How will He speak to me?"

Praying in Christ's Character

The disciples' selfish expressions stand in stark contrast to Jesus' concern for others. They quarreled about which of them was regarded as greatest (see Luke 9:46; 22:24); James and John wanted to sit on His right hand (see Matt. 20:20-28). Not one selfish thought or action is recorded of Jesus. He owned little and never expressed a desire for anything other than His Father's will.

Jesus' prayer for Himself occupies 5 of the 26 verses in the High-Priestly prayer of John 17, so a certain kind of thought for self is permissible. Yet even in these 5 verses He is praying for the restoration of a right order that will make salvation available for all people (see vv. 2-3). In other words, His prayer for Himself carries within it benevolence for others. The 21 other verses are devoted to prayer for His disciples and for those who would come afterward. Paul commented, "Even Christ did not please Himself" (Rom. 15:3). The noblest description of Christ's unselfishness is in 2 Corinthians 8:9: "You know the grace of our Lord Jesus Christ, that though He was rich, yet for your sake He became poor, that you through His poverty might become rich."

This ideal became the standard for the believers in the New Testament church. Jesus had redefined who our neighbor is (see Luke 10:30-37). He had placed the command to love one's neighbor second to the command to love God (see Mark 12:28-31). The continuing unfolding of new revelation would be consistent with Jesus' life and teaching. Paul enjoined the Corinthians, "Let no one seek his own good, but that of his neighbor" (1 Cor. 10:24).

Our prayer must match our lives, and our lives should match our prayer. Repeatedly, Paul poured out his heart in his prayers for the churches, and his travels and work with them match his prayers. He refused to accept money from the Corinthian church (see 1 Cor. 9:1-15; 2 Cor. 11:7-9), but he taught them, preached to them, and prayed for them. He told them, "I also please all men in all things, not seeking my own profit, but the profit of the many, that they may be saved" (1 Cor. 10:33). We must always pray in Christ's character. That character is perfectly seen in the person of Christ; it is reflected in Paul and is to be reflected in all disciples who seek the glory of God and the coming of His kingdom.

Our prayer must match our lives, and our lives should match our prayer.

One problem we perpetually face as humans is the dilemma of moving rather awkwardly toward the throne from which we are to rule. Full dominion has not yet been restored (see Rom. 8:18-25), and waiting while we learn is part of our training. Endurance is the temporal expression of immutability, and we are to become like God in all aspects of character.

That is the basic purpose of prayer. We become like what or whom we spend time with. In fellowship with God we are learning His character and are expressing His character to the world. That is why He honors prayer—so that His character will indeed be

The grandest, holiest, most dynamic events in the cosmos are being brought about through prayer.

expressed to the world. That is why prayer is, after all, the most powerful force available to Christians. We are part of a plan grander than the greatest minds can conceive, holier than any prophet can describe, richer than human language can explore. The grandest, holiest, most dynamic events in the cosmos are being brought about through prayer. And it is being done by seemingly normal, average, ordinary people who will someday sit on thrones of unimaginable authority and dominion.

Turn to the first learning activity in chapter 1 (pp. 7–8). You wrote a question about prayer that you wanted to be answered during your study. Write an answer to your question, based on what you have learned.

_____

_____

You also stated what you hoped to gain from this study. Did you achieve your goal? ❑ Yes ❑ No

Remember, God's truth is not just something to know; it is also to be put into practice. May God bless your life abundantly as you enjoy a richer, more intimate prayer life with Him.

You may wish to study additional courses by Dr. Hunt. They are listed, along with other discipleship studies, in "For Further Study" on page 143.

[1]Vance Havner, in *Southern Baptist Preaching Yesterday,* comp. R. Earl Allen and Joel Gregory (Nashville: Broadman Press, 1991), 218.
[2]B. H. Carroll, *Messages on Prayer* (Nashville: Broadman Press, 1942), 32.
[3]Robert Murray McCheyne, *Sermons of Robert Murray McCheyne* (London: The Banner of Truth Trust, 1961),17.
[4]Billy Graham, *Answers to Life's Problems: Guidance, Inspiration and Hope for the Challenges of Today* (n.p.: W Publishing Group, 1988), 162.
[5]E. F. Hallock, *Always in Prayer* (Nashville: Broadman Press, 1966), 69.
[6]L. R. Scarborough, *With Christ After the Lost* (Nashville: Broadman Press, 1952), 19.

For Further Study

Blackaby, Henry T., and Claude V. King. *Experiencing God.* Nashville: LifeWay Press, 1990.

Franklin, John, comp. *A House of Prayer: Prayer Ministries in Your Church.* Nashville: LifeWay Press, 1999.

Hemphill, Ken. *The Prayer of Jesus.* Nashville: LifeWay Press, 2002.

Hunt, T. W., and Claude V. King. *In God's Presence: Your Daily Guide to a Meaningful Prayer Life.* Nashville: LifeWay Press, 1994.

Hunt, T. W., and Claude V. King. *The Mind of Christ.* Nashville: LifeWay Press, 1997.

Hunt, T. W., and Catherine Walker. *Disciple's Prayer Life: Walking in Fellowship with God.* Nashville: LifeWay Press, 1997.

Hunt, T. W., and Melana Hunt Monroe. *From Heaven's View: God Bringing His Children to Glory.* Nashville: LifeWay Press, 2002.

McQuilkin, Robertson. *Life in the Spirit.* Nashville: LifeWay Press, 1997.

Thompson, Larry L. *Watchman Prayer Guide* and *Watchman Planning Kit.* Nashville: LifeWay Press, 1992.

Willis, Avery T., Jr. *MasterLife.* Nashville: LifeWay Press, 1996–97.

Willis, Avery T., Jr., and Henry T. Blackaby. *On Mission with God.* Nashville: LifeWay Press, 2001.

Willis, Avery T., Jr., and J. David Carter. *Day by Day in God's Kingdom: A Discipleship Journal.* Nashville: LifeWay Press, 1997.

CHRISTIAN GROWTH STUDY PLAN

Preparing Christians to Serve

In the **Christian Growth Study Plan (formerly the Church Study Course)** this book, *The Life-Changing Power of Prayer,* is a resource for course credit in the subject area Prayer in the Christian Growth category of diploma plans. To receive credit, read the book; complete the learning activities; show your work to your pastor, a staff member, or a church leader; then complete the following information. This page may be duplicated. Send the completed page to:

Christian Growth Study Plan
One LifeWay Plaza; Nashville, TN 37234-0117
Fax: (615) 251-5067; email: *cgspnet@lifeway.com*
For information about the Christian Growth Study Plan, refer to the current *Christian Growth Study Plan Catalog.* Your church office may have a copy. If not, request a free copy from the Christian Growth Study Plan office, (615) 251-2525. Also available online at *www.lifeway.com/cgsp/catalog.*

THE LIFE-CHANGING POWER OF PRAYER
COURSE NUMBER: CG-0789

PARTICIPANT INFORMATION

Social Security Number (USA ONLY-optional)	Personal CGSP Number*	Date of Birth (MONTH, DAY, YEAR)

Name (First, Middle, Last)	Home Phone

Address (Street, Route, or P.O. Box)	City, State, or Province	Zip/Postal Code

CHURCH INFORMATION

Church Name

Address (Street, Route, or P.O. Box)	City, State, or Province	Zip/Postal Code

CHANGE REQUEST ONLY

☐ Former Name		
☐ Former Address	City, State, or Province	Zip/Postal Code
☐ Former Church	City, State, or Province	Zip/Postal Code

Signature of Pastor, Conference Leader, or Other Church Leader	Date

*New participants are requested but not required to give SS# and date of birth. Existing participants, please give CGSP# when using SS# for the first time. Thereafter, only one ID# is required. **Mail to:** Christian Growth Study Plan, One LifeWay Plaza, Nashville, TN 37234-0117. Fax: (615)251-5067.

Rev. 5-02